Using Open Source Systems for Digital Libraries

Art Rhyno

LIBRARIES
U N L I M I T E D

A Member of the Greenwood Publishing Group

Westport, Connecticut • London

Library of Congress Cataloging-in-Publication Data

Rhyno, Art.
  Using open source systems for digital libraries / Art Rhyno.
    p. cm.
  ISBN: 1–59158–065–X (alk. paper)
    1. Digital libraries—Computer programs. 2. Open source software. I. Title.
  ZA4080.R48 2004
  025'.00285—dc22   2003058906

British Library Cataloguing in Publication Data is available.

Library of Congress Catalog Card Number: 2003058906
ISBN: 1–59158–065–X

First published in 2004

Libraries Unlimited, 88 Post Road West, Westport, CT 06881
A Member of the Greenwood Publishing Group, Inc.
www.lu.com

Printed in the United States of America

The paper used in this book complies with the
Permanent Paper Standard issued by the National
Information Standards Organization (Z39.48–1984).

10   9   8   7   6   5   4   3   2   1

Contents

Preface

My first interaction with a library was through the New Glasgow branch of the Pictou-Antigonish Regional Library System in Nova Scotia, a province on Canada's east coast. As I grew up in the small village of Coalburn, one of many rural areas served by this system, the public library seemed like an entry point to an endless set of exciting new worlds. The library was a place where even coal miners' sons and daughters could sail with Vikings, walk with dinosaurs, travel to distant lands, and explore the heavens.

Despite the amazing advances in technology and communications that have occurred in the last few decades, the intersection of inquisitive minds and the sea of content captured within a library collection, whether analog or digital, remains the point where the power of a thousand suns occurs. The technology in the process is important, and its role in extending collections around the planet is exciting, but in the end, it is subservient and perhaps even unremarkable when compared to this meeting point. No amount of hardware and software can match the wonder of human thought embarking on the hidden and well-trod pathways of the past or using these pathways to create something new.

This book is a direct result of having my first library card and reflects a genuine awe of the power of libraries. I am fortunate to have been able to spend a large part of my personal and working life in libraries, and luckier still to have the opportunity to combine a passion for technology with the time-honored mantle of librarianship. Anyone who has ever lived in Nova Scotia, particularly in the numerous Scottish-influenced areas of the province, will recognize that pragmatism sometimes seems to be engrained in the character of anyone raised there. This book attempts to be a practical guide to using open source software for building digital libraries. It is my hope that you will be able to use this book for achievable projects involving useful, and perhaps even inspiring, collections.

To that end, I have attempted to provide a starting point for some key technologies underlying digital libraries, a roundup of associated tools that make these technologies usable, and a close view of the areas in which additional information on a specific technology or tool opens the door to making full use of it for servicing a digital collection. I have tried not to replicate a lot of what is publicly available material on digital libraries, and I invite you to visit the associated Web site for this book where the references contained here are kept up-to-date.[1]

Defining solutions for building digital libraries has been compared to "nailing Jello to a wall," and there is no doubt that this subject area is undergoing rapid change, even by the sometimes notoriously fickle whims of technology. I hope this book gives a running start for navigating among open source solutions for digital libraries, but be prepared for lots of maneuvering in moving through an implementation. It is a dull bookshelf indeed that holds but one type of book, and digital libraries share with physical libraries the premise that variations in structure, service points, and overall organization may be required to best serve the library's user community.

Yet this service to the library's community is at the core of digital libraries as much as it is for their physical counterparts. The tools here are presented to assist in the process of matching the community with the best content possible. There will be few tears shed if the tools for this activity continue to multiply and increase in functionality as fast as they can be described. Such is probably the unavoidable fate of software and related technologies in a world of global networks and Internet time.

Introduction

Digital libraries (DL) have become a major part of the mainstream library landscape, while open source software (OSS) has become a worldwide phenomenon. Like many trends fueled by emerging technologies, the definitions of *digital library* and *open source* tend to be fluid and subject to some debate. For the purposes of this book, the adopted definition for digital libraries comes from a group of practitioners called the Digital Library Federation (DLF),[1] a consortium of libraries and related agencies that are extensively engaged in the use of electronic information technologies to extend their collections and services. The DLF has established a working definition that reads as follows:

> Digital libraries are organizations that provide the resources, including the specialized staff, to select, structure, offer intellectual access to, interpret, distribute, preserve the integrity of, and ensure the persistence over time of collections of digital works so that they are readily and economically available for use by a defined community or set of communities.[2]

Other attempts to define digital libraries are readily available,[3] and there is a substantial body of work on the underlying assumptions and goals of digital library services,[4] but the DLF statement captures the essential notions of collaboration and community, the building blocks of libraries in any form. Whatever the variance in the meaning of *digital libraries,* there is common agreement that they are usually a significant undertaking and that the selection and collection-building skills required for digital libraries are a direct linkage to the activities libraries have traditionally carried out for their user communities.

Open source software also has a community connection. Although most OSS definitions focus on the availability of *source code,* that is, the statements of the programming language that make up the application or suite of applications, open source software is created and nurtured by a community, sometimes one consisting solely of software developers, sometimes application users, but most often, the community is a combination of both. The Open Source Initiative (OSI),[5] which holds the trademark to the term *open source software,* defines OSS not only in terms of the availability of the source code, but uses criteria that include free distribution of the application, as well as provision for the future use of the code in modifications and derived works without discrimination against the persons or groups involved.[6]

Eric Raymond's seminal work on OSS entitled *The Cathedral and the Bazaar* describes two fundamentally different software development styles, the "cathedral" model, representing most of the commercial world, versus the "bazaar" model of the open source world. Using extensive examples of how a young Finish graduate student named Linus Torvalds (and a worldwide group of volunteers) developed the Linux operating system in a free-ranging and open environment (the bazaar model), Raymond contrasts it with the more insular and closed cathedral model exemplified by many commercial products (such as Microsoft Office).[7]

Many of the assertions of *The Cathedral and the Bazaar,* including the now famous "given enough eyes, all bugs are shallow," are based on the idea that the Internet enables a large community of developers than can be applied to a project by even the largest companies. Open source software is often characterized as free software, but it is important to realize that it is distinctly different from freeware. An OSS application will normally be distributed with a license that governs its use and distribution, and it is considered a licensed system. Richard Stallman, a founder of the GNU Project (*GNU* stands for Gnu's Not UNIX) and a leading figure in the OSS world, identifies fours kinds of freedom for open source applications that are supported by the licensing:

- The freedom to run the program for any purpose (freedom 0).

- The freedom to study how the program works and adapt it to your needs (freedom 1). Access to the source code is a precondition for this.

- The freedom to redistribute copies so you can help your neighbor (freedom 2).

- The freedom to improve the program and release your improvements to the public so that the whole community benefits (freedom 3). Access to the source code is a precondition for this, too.[8]

This extensive notion of freedom as exemplified by Stallman's four levels has led to the recent use of the acronym FLOSS (Free/Libre and Open Source Software), which seems to be entering widespread use as a result of the title *Free/Libre and Open Source Software: Survey and Study* commissioned by the European Commission and published in July 2002.[9] OSS is still the more familiar acronym for open source initiatives at the time of this writing, so it is used throughout the text, but it's possible that FLOSS may soon be the most widely deployed description of tools arising from the open source movement.

Table I.1 shows the most common OSS licenses and describes most of the licenses behind all the systems found in this book. OSS licenses are of particular concern if a system is going to be repackaged and made available to others in a commercial setting. For many digital library projects, the OSS license stands a very good chance of being acceptable to the organizations involved, but it is always important to understand the restrictions on the software, OSS or otherwise, before committing to using any system for a project.

Table I.1. Popular Open Source Software Licenses

License	Description
GNU General Public License (GPL)[10]	Perhaps the most common of OSS licenses, the GPL implements a concept known as "copyleft" that attempts to negate copyright for the purposes of collaborative software development. Under the GPL license, the code for a GPL-licensed application can be used anywhere in any situation; it can be distributed to anyone as long as the code is included and the GPL license is retained; and anyone can create a derivative work from the code and redistribute it, as long as the resulting code is made available and also licensed under the GPL.
Creative Commons[11]	Creative Commons licensing is similar to that of the GPL, but is not designed around software. The Creative Commons license is for other creative works such as music and film, though it is sometimes utilized within software projects.[12]
GNU Lesser General Public License (LGPL),[13] Artistic License[14]	LGPL is normally used to designate source code that can be used by applications for which a charge is levied, so that this code can be used in commercial products; hence, "lesser." The Artistic License also attempts to mitigate the fear of using code for commercial purposes.
Berkley System Distribution (BSD) license,[15] Apache Software License,[16] MIT License,[17] NCSA License[18]	The BSD license is the basis for many other licenses, including those listed here. It mainly concerns whether the copyright of the code is recognized as belonging with the creators and whether this copyright is promulgated to applications built with the source code. The BSD license, like almost all OSS licenses, also specifies that the copyright holder is not liable for the consequences of using the source code.
Mozilla Public License (MPL or MozPL),[19] Netscape Public License (NPL)[20]	The MPL is similar to the BSD license, but has special provision for ensuring that modifications are reported back to the license holders. The NPL grants special rights to server-side applications, for which the code does not have to be made available.
OCLC Research Public License[21]	Like the MPL, the OCLC license ensures that modifications are reported back to OCLC if the intent is to redistribute the changes externally.

In addition to a long history of dealing with licensed content and related issues, libraries have a natural synergy with the open source movement. Library collections, library staff, and even the physical structures usually are available to a wide community of users on a nonprofit, publicly funded basis. Libraries are also, like most organizations, frequent users of open source software, though staff in libraries and other organizations may often be unaware of how many mainstream library services are delivered using OSS options.

This is largely because the greatest participation in open source software for most computer users occurs over the Internet, not only because this infrastructure is built on OSS applications, but also because the Internet has become so ubiquitous that much of its underlying technology is taken for granted. Some of the pillars of Internet computing, such as the sendmail mail server and BIND, the software that runs the Domain Name System (DNS) that locates network addresses, are OSS applications. Apache, the most popular Web server in the world, is both maintained and enhanced through an open source model, and many library Web services run on Linux, one of the software world's highest- performance operating systems. Out of all the OSS systems available, it is Linux that is the most recognizable and that is most often identified as the poster child of OSS.

The key term to connect digital libraries and OSS is *open*. In fact, digital libraries are sometimes referred to as open digital libraries (ODL), and "open" models, such as open archives, have emerged at every level of intellectual property sharing.[22] Libraries have derived much support from the premise that an open society is dependent on the free exchange of ideas and opinions, as well as the existence of an informed citizenry. Digital libraries and open source software are a natural outgrowth of the open models of exchange that help societies grow and prosper.

How This Book Is Organized

This book attempts to move logically through the steps and associated software involved in building a digital library. An organization often may be the recipient of a process that has already shifted the digital library in a certain direction, such as suddenly being handed a collection of graphics files or scientific data, so it is recognized that digital libraries may have different starting points. Each chapter can be read in isolation, but the groundwork for a particular topic sometimes might have been sketched out in a previous chapter. Some topics, such as scripting languages, can easily be plucked out of the rest, whereas other areas, particularly XML, are engrained in so many aspects of digital libraries that they appear almost everywhere. A brief overview of the chapters and the layout of the book follows.

Chapter 1, "Scoping Out Content for Digital Libraries: A Tale of Documents, Multimedia, and Metadata," covers some of the decisions that must be made for the content of digital collections and introduces Extensible Markup Language (XML), metadata, and related technologies for servicing this content.

Chapter 2 is entitled "Important Protocols for Digital Libraries and OSS Options for Using Them." Protocols are what make it possible for different computers and applications to talk to each other. This chapter provides an introduction to some protocols and associated software that are essential in constructing digital libraries, as well as a few that are emerging for services that can be built around digital libraries.

Content for digital libraries usually requires manipulation by several tools before it reaches a form in which it is ready for access and examination by the library's user community. Chapter 3, "OSS Authoring Tools for Digital Libraries," covers the most common types of tools that are necessary for creating the material that will be digitally housed in the library's collection.

Most digital collections will involve the use of XML, and Chapter 4, "OSS Tools for Manipulating and Transforming XML," provides an introduction to applications that will help realize XML's flexibility for delivering multiple formats for different audiences.

Relational database management systems (RDBMSs) are the most popular type of database tool for organizing data and represent a class of applications in which open source solutions are particularly strong. Chapter 5, "Open Source Relational Databases for Digital Libraries," examines why relational databases are useful and looks at setting up an application with the most successful OSS database in the world.

Although not as widely used as relational databases, object and XML databases can be an excellent match for digital library content. Chapter 6, "Object and XML Databases," focuses on the use of a popular object database–based system for XML content as well as an XML-specific database solution.

The concept of digital libraries has been around long enough so that mature systems have been built specifically for digital collections, and many of these systems are available as open source software. Chapter 7, "Built to Order: DL-Specific Systems," is a roundup of applications that are ready "out of the box" for building a digital library.

At some point, a digital library may need special processing for modifying content or providing additional services for the collection. Chapter 8, "Scripting Languages and Regular Expressions," contains a brief overview of the differences between scripting languages and traditional programming languages for these purposes and examines three of the most popular scripting options, as well as why their common support of regular expressions is a key factor in their success.

Resource sharing in digital libraries is important not only for the objects in a digital collection, but also for the technologies that underlie a digital library. The use of component-based systems and Web services for plugging digital libraries into each other as well as into mainstream services is examined in Chapter 9, "Plugging Digital Libraries into the Mainstream."

Chapter 10, "Long-Term Care and Feeding of Digital Libraries," examines issues surrounding the maintenance and service of an existing digital library. Some strategies for preservation of digital content are examined, and the chapter includes a brief overview of the preeminent model for the long-term storage of digital data.

Finally, "Further Resources: Digital Library and Open Source Resources on the Web," is an annotated list of resources for digital libraries and open source software, providing additional information on topics raised in this book.

Scoping Out Content for Digital Libraries: A Tale of Documents, Multimedia, and Metadata

Understanding Differences in Digital Objects

Curators of most digital libraries tend to be concerned primarily with providing access and management for digital material, or *objects,* which are broadly defined as electronic entities made meaningful by a computer or some other combination of hardware and software. It could be argued that all digital objects are fundamentally a series of ones and zeros in the same way that human beings are carbon-based life-forms, but it is much easier to work with a more refined notion of format that better reflects the requirements of the object in question. These requirements are what allow the object to be rendered in a way that humans can apply to their own considerable processing capabilities.

There are usually two types of objects in digital libraries. One is an object that is a surrogate for another object that exists in analog form, such as an electronic version of a rare book. The other type of object exists solely in digital form.[1] Such objects are either born digital or perhaps only an electronic surrogate exists; for example, a scanned image of a document that has since been lost. This distinction is not absolute; firmware, for example, may be modeled electronically, but the physical artifact embeds a digital existence. However, suffice it to say that the digital object attempts to either do justice to or be a "faithful facsimile" of the original entity.[2]

Digital objects, such as the objects in physical libraries, typically are organized into collections that reflect a common theme or purpose. One of the unique aspects of digital libraries is that these collections are not always defined by possession but rather by access. The user of a digital library often is unaware of what system or subsystem delivers the object being viewed, and these systems may lay virtually or physically well outside the organization's walls.

The life cycle of a DL project and the associated collections can be seen in Figure 1.1.

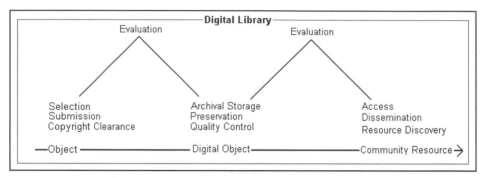

Figure 1.1. An object travels toward a digital existence in a DL project.
Much of the hard work may occur in the selection stage.

Note that a fundamental part of the process of building a digital library is evaluation. This book focuses on the selection and deployment of systems that underlie the process described in the illustration. These systems share the following characteristics:

- They are freely available or in the process of being made available with a recognized OSS license.

- They have been deployed in real life for real projects.

To navigate among the system options for digital libraries, it is essential to identify and define storage formats that best meet the needs of the collection the system(s) will house. Table 1.1 outlines some of the most common media types and formats following the guidelines made available by the Institute of Museum and Library Services (IMLS).[3]

In most cases, the key distinction for selecting a system largely concerns whether the collections will house documents or multimedia objects, or combinations of both. Documents, in this case, are considered structured or semistructured representations of materials that are stored and delivered as text. Some digital library projects classify all media types as documents, but for deploying systems for digital objects, a more pragmatic distinction is to follow the normal practice used in designing databases and to separate the world into document objects that consist primarily of text and others that are primarily multimedia, such as video. For example, collections consisting of diaries or manuscripts may be made available as both documents, in which electronic representations of text are made available as text, and multimedia, in which images of the pages along with sound clips are accessible.

A common theme in digital libraries is that even when collections consist of homogeneous objects, for example, an electronic text collection, there may be a need to utilize several different underlying systems to service the collection. For example, an external application to the digital library may be used to support keyword indexing for text stored on a Web server, and another might handle the automatic generation of JPEG (which stands for Joint Photographic Experts Group) images from Tagged Image File Format (TIFF) masters for multimedia stored in a database.

Table 1.1. Guidelines for Media and Formats

Content Type	Application	Formats
Alphanumeric data	Flat files, documents in proprietary formats, unstructured textual data	For preservation and migration purposes, data should be convertible to American Standard Code for Information Interchange (ASCII),[4] at the very least, and Unicode,[5] if dealing with a wide range of language materials. Comma-delimited ASCII, or portable format files recognized as de facto standards (e.g., SAS[6] and SPSS[7]) with enough information to reconstruct the original will be important for data sets.
	Encoded texts for networked presentation and exchange, structured documents	XML using documented DTDs or schema when possible (see the following). For example, the Text Encoding Initiative (TEI)[8] standard for full-text resources and the Encoded Archival Description (EAD)[9] for Finding Aids.
Image data	Digital or scanned line drawings, illustrated texts, paintings, illustrations	Archival masters likely to be TIFF files at color depth and pixelation appropriate for the application.[10] Delivery formats include JPEG, GIF, and other lossy but bandwidth-friendly formats.[11]
	Maps, physical artifacts	Proprietary wavelet-based compression formats such as MrSID[12] have been widely used, but JPEG 2000[13] now holds great promise.
Audio	Music, oral histories	Archival masters are likely to be Audio Interchange File Format (AIFF).[14]

(*Continued*)

Content Type	Application	Formats
Video	Moving-image files	MPEG and QuickTime are two widely used formats.[15] Delivery formats may use streaming technologies.[16]
Scientific data	Examples include GIS, CAD, molecular data	Evolving, scientific data presents special challenges because it often requires sophisticated and customized extraction tools. In general, scientific data should be as portable as possible, and the tools for manipulating this data should be maintained in tandem with the content.

The Further Resources section will allow you to explore in more depth the background technologies associated with the media and formats in Table 1.1. One format cuts across all media, however, and deserves special attention: Extensible Markup Language (XML).

The Role of XML

XML is possibly the most documented technology on earth, and with good reason. Almost any substantive technology, especially if used for the World Wide Web, now is expected to define its relationship with XML. The good news is that XML is based on simple and well-grounded concepts. Despite layers of complexity that may exist in some XML-related technologies, XML itself reflects a commonsense approach to dealing with text.

To understand XML, it is worth remembering that electronic materials have historically contained control codes or macros that cause the document to be formatted in a particular way. Generic coding, which began in the late 1960s, was an attempt to use descriptive tags, such as <heading>, instead of ones that were specific to a particular system or printer, such as <format-42>. Many credit the start of the generic-coding movement to a presentation made by William Tunnicliffe, chairman of the Graphic Communications Association (GCA) Composition Committee, during a meeting at the Canadian Government Printing Office on the separation of the information content of documents from their format. Around the same time, a New York book designer named Stanley Rice proposed the idea of a universal catalogue of parameterized editorial tags. Norman Scharpf, director of the GCA, recognized the significance of these trends and established a generic-coding project in the Composition Committee.[17]

The result of this activity was the Generalized Markup Language (GML), based on the generic-coding ideas of Rice and Tunnicliffe. Instead of just being a simple tagging scheme, however, GML introduced the concept of a formally defined document type with an explicit nested element structure, called a document type definition (DTD). This concept allowed for *validation,* in which documents could be checked to see whether they are constructed to match the appropriate format.

In 1978, the American National Standards Institute (ANSI) Committee on Information Processing established the Computer Languages for the Processing of Text Committee, a project for a text description language standard based on GML. The first working draft of Standard Generalized Markup Language (SGML) was published in 1980, and it quickly was adopted by large organizations, such as the U.S. military, to help manage and standardize the vast number of documents published internally, such as helicopter manuals.

Fast-Forward to the Web

In the late 1980s, when Tim Berners-Lee, the inventor of the World Wide Web, was looking for ideas on a markup language to support hypertext linking, he turned to SGML. The result was Hypertext Markup Language (HTML), a simple application of SGML, but one with powerful linking capabilities and timed with the growing popularity of the global network called the Internet.[18] Together, HTML and the Internet brought about the widest publishing system ever to be seen with the explosion of the Web.

HTML was an appropriate tool for creating simple documents, but HTML tags are almost totally concerned with presentation. This becomes a problem in the same way that <format-42> caused difficulties with early documents. For example, if a Web page contains HTML such as the following, a human reader could presumably tell that the content is a position paper:

```
<H1>Open Source Meets Digital Libraries Position Paper</H1>
```

However, if there were hundreds of documents that contained significant subject information, difficulty arises if some authors choose to use tags such as this:

```
<H3>Open Source Meets Digital Libraries—A Different Position Paper</H3>
```

If you want to use a program to extract subject information, or even if you just want consistency in subject assignment, it becomes difficult without a commonly used tag such as <subject> to mark or *delimit* where this information is contained. Most important, HTML is also a fixed set of tags, <subject> is not considered a valid HTML tag and cannot be added to the language without navigating the W3C committees and/or convincing browser maintainers that it is a good idea.

Another factor limiting HTML's flexibility for a large collection of materials is the separation of content and presentation, as important a principle for managing collections of documents today as it was in the 1960s. HTML mixes both together freely, which was fine for the early days of the Web, but as Web sites grew from containing several HTML documents to becoming the public virtual face of most organizations, there was a sense that a "webified" version of SGML was needed.

XML: HTML-Plus or SGML-Lite?

In 1998, the World Wide Web Consortium (W3C), the body that oversees Web standards, published the XML 1.0 recommendations. The standard was a greatly simplified version of SGML and was greeted with open enthusiasm, in part because harried Web administrators and publishers immediately recognized how useful XML would be. XML makes frequent appearances in this book, but for now, here are the aspects of XML that are essential to digital libraries:

- *XML is well formed.* DLs are very sensitive to scalability issues. Having a few tags with a missing < or /> may not be a big issue with a few HTML documents, but it becomes the bane of your existence when trying to maintain consistency and quality control for thousands of documents. XML is far less forgiving than HTML, and software is readily available to ensure that an XML document meets baseline requirements.

- *XML is well behaved.* DTDs were the original validation mechanism for XML content, but they are cryptic. A newer mechanism for validation that not only ensures that documents are consistent but that actually uses XML is XML Schema. Table 1.2 shows a DTD and schema side by side. Almost the only reason to use a DTD any more is if a schema is not available or the software supports only DTDs. At the time of this writing, DTDs are still far more common than XML schemas, but this is changing. Although DTDs and schemas are useful on their own, their greatest value comes when they are defined and shared by a community. Identifying or authoring the appropriate DTD or schema is one of the most important steps in putting together a digital collection because it establishes consistency in the content that will help in sharing content and in future migrations.

- *XML is the key to an amazing quantity and diversity of DL tools and software.* Eric Raymond notes that one of the important traits of a great programmer is "constructive laziness." From a practical perspective, XML allows you to leverage a worldwide community's efforts in defining tools and applications for managing content. Even if you came to the conclusion that XML is the most despicable technology in the world, the most gifted and well-funded DL project team would be hard pressed to build even a fraction of the infrastructure into which XML immediately taps.

Table 1.2. Comparison of a Document Type Definition (DTD)
and an Extensible Markup Language (XML) Schema

XML Example – business cards for Ancient Greeks

```
<author xmlns="http://authors.org">
   <name>Homer</name>
   <title>CEO, Storytellers Unlimited</title>
   <email>homer@ancientworld.org</email>
   <phone>(000) 000-0000</phone>
</author>
```

DTD Version	XML Schema Version

`<!DOCTYPE author [`
`  <!ELEMENT author`
`(name,title,email,phone)>`
`  <!ELEMENT name (#PCDATA)>`
`  <!ELEMENT title (#PCDATA)>`
`  <!ELEMENT email (#PCDATA)>`
`  <!ELEMENT phone (#PCDATA)>`
`]>`
 	
The DTD is somewhat cryptic, the !ELEMENT author defines the element "author" as having four elements: "name,title,email, phone".
 	
!ELEMENT name (in line 4) defines the "name" element to be of the type PCDATA which means it consists of character data and so on.
	`<schema xmlns="http://www.w3.org/2001/`
	`XMLSchema"`
	`    xmlns:a="http://authors.org"`
	`    targetNamespace="http://authors.org">`
	`<element name="author" type="a:author_type"/>`
	`<element name="name" type="string"/>`
	`<element name="title" type="string"/>`
	`<element name="email" type="string"/>`
	`<element name="phone" type="string"/>`
	
	`<complexType name="author_type">`
	` <sequence>`
	`  <element ref="a:name"/>`
	`  <element ref="a:title"/>`
	`  <element ref="a:email"/>`
	`  <element ref="a:phone" minOccurs="0"/>`
	` </sequence>`
	`</complexType>`
	`</schema>`
	
	The XML Schema language is recognized by the namespace http://www.w3.org/2001/XMLSchema.
	
	XML Schema is normally far more verbose than a DTD, and in this case a complexType element is used to bring together our elements. Note the use of string instead of PCDATA.

XML not only is used for structuring documents and other types of content. It has become the preferred format for configuration files and describing all manner of activities, from mapping moves in chess games to mind reading.[19] In addition to its usefulness in structuring the content of a DL, XML also shines for working with the descriptive data, or *metadata,* associated with a digital collection, which, like XML, deserves some special attention.

Metadata and Access Levels

Metadata has been popularized as "data about data" and consists of the elements necessary to describe an object, with provision for supporting the "discovery" of the object, a process often called *resource discovery*. Metadata is usually categorized according to three types:

- *Administrative.* Metadata used for managing and preserving objects in the repository. This metadata might be concerned with acquisition information, rights and use tracking, selection criteria for digitization, version control, and audit trails.

- *Structural.* Metadata used primarily to capture the structure and organization of an object. Structural metadata includes descriptions such as page and chapter layouts.

- *Descriptive.* Metadata used for resource discovery of objects. Library metadata is largely descriptive with generally agreed upon standard forms of description and controlled vocabularies and data formats (along with organizations and procedures for maintaining such standards).

In all cases, metadata can be considered value-added information used to arrange, describe, track, and otherwise enhance access to information objects. Anne Gilliland-Swetland, a prolific writer on metadata topics, includes the following among the functions of metadata:

- Certifying the authenticity and degree of completeness of the content

- Establishing and documenting the context of the content

- Identifying and exploiting the structural relationships that exist between and within information objects

- Providing a range of intellectual access points for an increasingly diverse range of users

- Providing some of the information an information professional might have provided in a physical reference or research setting[20]

Metadata probably becomes most useful if it contains enough description of a resource to allow a user to assess the resource's potential utility without having to retrieve the object or visit its location. One of the simplest and most common metadata formats is the Dublin Core metadata set designed by a broadly representative group from the library, research, and academic communities, as well as from industry. This set takes it name from a workshop hosted by OCLC in Dublin, Ohio, in 1995.

The Dublin Core metadata set consists of 15 elements (see Table 1.3) considered to be straightforward enough to be generated by Web authors, yet that can be expanded or *qualified* to incorporate controlled vocabularies and additional specificity for the given element.

Table 1.3. The Dublin Core Metadata Set

Element	Description
Title	The name given to a resource
Creator	The person(s) or organization(s) primarily responsible for the intellectual content of the resource
Subject	Topic of the resource, or keywords, phrases, or classification descriptors that describe the subject or content of the resource
Description	A textual description of the content of the resource
Publisher	The entity responsible for making the resource available in its present form, such as a library or university department
Other Contributors	Person(s) or organization(s) in addition to those specified in the Creator element who have made significant but secondary intellectual contributions to the resource
Date	The date the resource was made available in its present form
Resource Type	The category of the resource, such as home page, usually chosen from an enumerated list of types
Format	The data representation of the resource, such as ASCII or JPEG image, assigned from enumerated lists such as MIME
Resource Identifier	String or number used to uniquely identify the resource, such as URL
Source	The work from which this resource is delivered, if applicable
Language	Language(s) of the intellectual content of the resource
Relation	Relationship to other resources
Coverage	The spatial locations and temporal durations characteristics of the resource
Rights Management	Intended to be a link (a URL or other suitable URI as appropriate) to a copyright notice or form of rights-management statement

For example, here are some <META> tags using Dublin Core elements that might be found in an HTML page for this book:

```
<link rel="schema.DC" href="http://purl.org/dc/elements/1.0/">
<META name="DC.title" content="Using Open Source Systems for Digital
Libraries">
<META name="DC.author" content="Art Rhyno">
<META NAME="DC.Date.modified" SCHEME="W3C-DTF"
CONTENT="2003-04-28">
```

Note the use of SCHEME in the example; it is used to qualify the content to indicate that the date follows a certain format and is an example of qualified Dublin Core, where an element is refined or further described by using a recognized or prescribed value or format. *Scheme* is a term often used to designate a particular format or set of metadata.

In addition to Dublin Core, there are many other metadata standards, including the well-known Machine Readable Cataloguing (MARC),[21] which a number of initiatives have moved into the XML world.[22] A typical reason to go beyond Dublin Core is to support much deeper levels of description than Dublin Core allows.

Metadata is probably the single most valuable item you will add to a collection beyond the objects themselves, and the selection of an appropriate standard is comparable to choosing the right format for storing content. Table 1.4 lists several of the most common metadata schemes beyond Dublin Core and MARC.

One standard of particular importance for metadata in digital libraries is the Metadata Encoding and Transmission Standard (METS).[23] METS, an initiative from the Digital Library Federation based on experience from the Library of Congress's Making of America 2 (MOA2) project, encapsulates the different types of metadata associated with a digital object (see Figure 1.2). METS brings together multiple forms of administrative and descriptive metadata, along with a structure to specify the different actions or *behaviors* associated with the object, such as linking to a service that supplies thumbnails of an image.

One of the key features of METS is that it allows a list of files to be maintained that comprise a single electronic version of a digital object. For example, an object that is available as a TEI-encoded manuscript and a multipage TIFF format might be specified as follows:

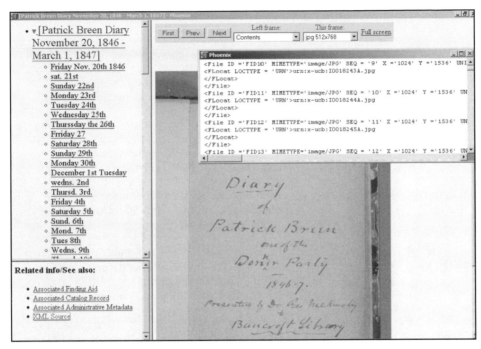

Figure 1.2. MOA2 Viewer developed by the Library Systems Office at University of California at Berkeley. METS is the successor to MOA2, and this is an example of how multiple files are attached to one object. Notice the XML source link has been opened.

```
<fileGrp>
  <fileGrp ID="version1">
    <file ID="patrick001" MIMETYPE="application/xml" SIZE="689445"
      CREATED="2003-03-17">
    <FLocat LOCTYPE="URL">
    http://www.dl.org/manuscripts/patrick.xml
    </FLocat>
    </file>
  </fileGrp>
  <fileGrp ID="version2">
    <file ID="patrick002" MIMETYPE="image/tiff" SIZE="9234567"
      CREATED="2003-03-17">
    <FLocat LOCTYPE="URL">
    http://www.dl.org/manuscripts/patrick.tiff
    </FLocat>
    </file>
  </fileGrp>
</fileGrp>
```

Table 1.4. Listing of Metadata Schemes

Metadata Scheme	Description
Global Information Locator Service (GILS)	A standard for governments and other organizations to describe collections.
Content Standard for Digital Geospatial Metadata (CSDGM)	A common set of terminology and definitions for the documentation of digital geospatial data. The standard establishes the names and appropriate use of data elements.
Learning Object Metadata (LOM)	Produced by the IEEE Learning Technology Standards Committee (LTSC). LOM is widely used for education objects.
Online Information exchange (ONIX)	ONIX is primarily used for publisher-generated metadata. It includes similar data elements to MARC such as author, title, and ISBN information, as well as such information as cover images and reviews.
Gateway to Educational Materials (GEM)	Based on Dublin Core, GEM includes a number of controlled vocabularies for subject, resource type, pedagogy, audience, and format.

METS has emerged as one of the most comprehensive solutions for metadata, while at the same time providing for a minimum use of unqualified Dublin Core for simple metadata support. Regardless of which type of metadata is selected for a project, it is a bridge to the future for digital collections. Metadata is what will help make it possible to understand objects in the collection if the social and environmental context for the objects is lost.

XML + Metadata = The Semantic Web?

It would be difficult to treat XML and metadata in the same chapter without some examination of the so-called Semantic Web. The Semantic Web has been described as a vision of the Web that goes beyond billions of linked Web documents waiting to be indexed by global search engines; it is a Web in which the semantics, or meaning behind the content, can be utilized in a meaningful way.[24] To some, this hearkens back to the failed promises of artificial intelligence computing and the nondelivery of systems that were supposed to work out the family's budget and intelligently order groceries for the week. The W3C's extensive work on the Semantic Web has even been characterized as taking place with a "pie-in-the-sky" attitude that has obscured and detracted from much-needed Web standardization efforts.[25]

The first real manifestation of the W3C's semantic work was the publication of the Resource Description Framework (RDF)[26] specification for encoding and sharing metadata. The premise of RDF is that metadata consists of statements or *assertions* about a resource. In RDF parlance, these are called *triples*. For example, the statement "Tim Severin is the creator of *The Brendan Voyage*" consists of three parts (Tim Severin, creator, *The Brendan Voyage*) and can be written in XML as follows:

```
<rdf:RDF
  xmlns:rdf="http://www.w3.org/TR/WD-rdf-syntax#"
  xmlns:dc="http://purl.org/dc/elements/1.0/">
  rdf:Description rdf:about="http://address_for_Brendan_voyage">
  <dc:Creator>
    Tim Severin
  </dc:Creator>
</rdf:RDF>
```

RDF specifies that every part of this assertion can be assigned a Uniform Resource Indicator (URI), much like a Uniform Resource Locator (URL) but different in the sense that it doesn't have to map to a real Web address and can represent concepts ("Creator"), living entities ("Tim Severin"), and anything else in the known and imagined universe, from animals to laundry lists. The *dc* in the example is for "Dublin Core," which is associated with a special URI called a *namespace* (purl.org/dc/elements/1.0/) that, in turn, is associated with a set of metadata elements. On its own, this is somewhat useful, but one of the most compelling aspects of RDF is combining elements from different metadata sets. If a digital collection employed a set of elements specifying a type of genre system, for example, a namespace (xmlns) reference could be inserted to include the rating as shown:

```
<rdf:RDF
  xmlns:rdf="http://www.w3.org/TR/WD-rdf-syntax#"
  xmlns:dc="http://purl.org/dc/elements/1.0/"
  xmlns:ar="http://www.for.me/ar/genres/0.1/">
  rdf:Description rdf:about="http://address_for_Brendan_voyage">
  <ar:GenreDescription>
    Travel Story
  </ar:GenreDescription>
  <dc:Creator>
    Tim Severin
  </dc:Creator>
</rdf:RDF>
```

As suggested by the example, RDF's rendering in XML is somewhat convoluted, and many consider RDF's biggest flaw to be its inelegant syntax. Tim Berners-Lee has proposed a simpler syntax for RDF called Notation 3, which results in triples such as the following:

```
:tim :creator "The Brendan Voyage"
```

Others also have made attempts to mitigate RDF's syntax,[27] but this is far from the only stumbling block on the way to the Semantic Web. Another difficulty with the Semantic Web is that going beyond assertions to supporting any high level of inferences, when a computer can automatically pull together concepts, really requires some understanding of RDF Schema and Ontology Languages such as DAML+OIL.[28]

RDF Schema allows concepts to be specified and related; for example, specifying that a "writer" is a type of "creator." Ontologies are also formal representations of relationships, but languages such as DAML+OIL differ from RDF Schema by supplying more types. For example, using Notation 3, we could have this relationship:

```
dc:Creator daml:equivalentTo red:PreparerName  .
```

This would allow a program to infer that a real estate agreement identified with the PreparerName element from the Real Estate Data (red) Consortium schema is equivalent to Creator from Dublin Core using the equivalentTo property from DAML+OIL. This means that in addition to titles of works that the author has written, a user of a digital library also could receive documents that represent the author's activities as a lawyer.

TAP and Topic Maps

Another initiative for the Semantic Web comes from a partnership of the Knowledge Systems Laboratory at Stanford University, the Knowledge Management Group of IBM, and the W3C's Semantic Web Advanced Development Initiatives team. Called TAP,[29] this project seeks to provide a uniform view of data by using a construct called GetData, which can be applied to a knowledge base (a database that contains questions and answers). The format of GetData is expressed as follows:

```
GetData(<resource>,<property>)=>value
```

This allows queries such as this, which asks for the location of Paris by using a common description or *property type* understood by both parties, in this case, locatedIn:

```
GetData(<Paris>,locatedIn)
```

The result is this:

```
=><France>
```

TAP works by attempting to leverage a common vocabulary for sharing information, for example, "city," with the RDF notion of URIs for resources, such as tap.stanford.edu/data/CityParis. Using an OSS system created with Apache, TAP allows sites to share and add terms for identifying objects, so that when different identifiers are used for an object such as a rare manuscript of *Beowulf,* the uniting description could be of the form *A Manuscript Whose Title Is Beowulf* instead of one site trying to determine whether www.dl.org/manuscripts/id0004 is a match for its own www.otherdl.org/data/ij009. In other words, the resource is referenced using *common descriptions* from the shared vocabulary.

Topic Maps[30] also represent an intriguing use of the Semantic Web. The central notion of Topic Maps is not a resource that is the object of *assertions,* but instead that the world is based on *topics.* Anything can be a topic and can incorporate other topics, including the works of Shakespeare and the notions of truth and love. Probably the key difference between Topic Maps and RDF is that topics can be much more abstract. Like RDF, Topic Maps can be expressed in XML and may have some utility as a data model for expressing associations between resources. For example, a Topic Map could be used to show that *The Brendan Voyage* is based on the story of the voyage of Saint Brendan to the New World.

```
<topic id="saint_brendan">
  <instanceOf>
    <topicRef xlink:href="#travel_log"/>
  </instanceOf>
  <baseName>
    <baseNameString>The Brendan Voyage</baseNameString>
  </baseName>
  <occurance>
    <instanceOf>
      <topicRef xlink:href="#based_on"/>
    </instanceOf>
    <resourceRef xlink:href="http://www.dl.org/brendan_manuscript"/>
  </occurance>
</topic>
```

Here, the association `based_on` is manifested in the resource link designated by `resourceRef` for the original Saint Brendan story. Whether this is more elegant than expressing the information in RDF is debatable, but Topic Maps may provide some additional semantic wiring for bringing together resources based on relationships that are not evident in the resource.

RDF and Topic Maps are very similar in the sense of being dependent on software to justify the amount of effort required to express information in either data model. A number of intriguing RDF-based databases, such as rdfDB,[31] are available, and some of the visualization tools[32] for Topic Maps hold promise for unique ways of navigating digital collections. Edutella, a peer-to-peer (P2P) project based on the JXTA project from Sun, is an OSS system using RDF to locate educational resources and represents a possible meeting point for the Semantic Web and education objects.[33]

For digital libraries, the value of the Semantic Web may have less to do with traditional information retrieval than expressing information that is awkward or impossible with traditional approaches to metadata. The Semantic Web may also be useful for working with resources that don't lend themselves to familiar information retrieval scenarios. Scientific data sets, for example, often do not have access points that translate well to "bibliographic-like" descriptions, and they bring in a multitude of concepts that may be critical for the associated resource communities. DNA models, solar wind movements, and other types of scientific data often require specialized query languages. The Semantic Web may help address the complexity of the semantics of these kinds of data so that this level of description need not be crammed into a lowest common denominator metadata scheme.

Putting It All Together

The content of digital libraries can vary greatly, particularly in media type. XML and metadata are key enablers for realizing the value of digital collections regardless of the underlying format. The Semantic Web could eventually build on metadata to express information about objects in digital libraries in new ways. The Semantic Web may be far less audacious in practice than in concept, and it could be an important tool for providing services for the growing stream of diverse content that will be housed in digital collections.

Important Protocols for Digital Libraries and OSS Options for Using Them

Digital libraries usually are called on to communicate with many different external systems. These duties can range from delivering Web-based interfaces for remote users to exposing content to third-party applications. Certain interactions are so common or have so many requirements that a protocol has been established for standardizing and streamlining the process. A *protocol* is a set of ground rules for how systems carry out specific activities. Protocols often define which format and syntax systems use for exchanging information and what one system must indicate to another before any data is made available.

A simple example of a protocol is the rules we follow when we address a letter (as in Figure 2.1). The first line usually contains the name of the person or organization to whom the letter is being sent. The next line or two contains the street name and building number, followed by a line with the city, state or province, and zip/postal code. Finally, if we are sending something to another country, the last line contains the country name. This protocol, when properly implemented, allows the correct delivery of billions of pieces of mail annually.

Digital Library Contact
14 DL Street
Digiville, MA
10042

Figure 2.1. The address on the envelope ensures that the letter will be delivered to the right location.

Protocols make up a large part of what happens on a network. When you turn on your computer, for example, you likely are interacting with several protocols standardizing actions as simple as accessing a shared drive or using a network printer. Not surprisingly, an enormous number of protocols can underlie digital library functionality, but in this book we limit our scope to the protocols that represent some fundamental plumbing for DL projects.

HTTP

The Hypertext Transfer Protocol (HTTP) powers the Web and is the protocol that most Web users interact with when using a Web browser. HTTP is easy to overlook, but digital libraries are so closely associated with the Web that it is well worth examining this, one of the most critical protocols on which the Web is dependent.[1]

At the most basic level, HTTP is used to exchange files (text, graphic images, sound, video, and other multimedia files) on the World Wide Web. It is an application protocol for the Transmission Control Protocol/Internet Protocol (TCP/IP)[2] suite of protocols (which is the basis for all information exchange on the Internet). A Web server machine provides an HTTP *daemon,* which is UNIX parlance for a program that runs on its own in the background. The HTTP daemon spends all of its time waiting for HTTP requests on a network at a certain channel, or *port,* an internal mechanism identified by a number the operating system uses to direct network traffic. By default, HTTP daemons use port 80, and traffic on this port is usually expected to be Web traffic.

Web browsers have become full-featured applications for e-mail and many other functions, but they are primarily HTTP clients, responsible for letting a computer user send requests to server machines for content using HTTP.

An HTTP request is submitted to the server by opening a Uniform Resource Indicator (URI) or clicking a hypertext link, at which point the browser builds an HTTP request and sends it to the address indicated by the URI. A specific form of a URI, called a Uniform Resource Locator (URL), normally is used to indicate the specific server being called. The URL specifies the protocol (http, ftp) or scheme (mailto) associated with the request, as well as the location of the machine to which the request should be directed. URLs are by far the most commonly used form of URI, but another form is the Uniform Resource Name (URN), an identifier that is independent of the location of a resource.

URNs are *resolved* to determine the location of a resource; for example, the Corporation of National Research Initiatives (CNRI) has developed a URN system called "handles"[3] that involves a registry and distributed resolving services so that a globally unique identifier or *handle,* known as a digital object identifier (DOI), can be assigned to a resource and be consistent across changes in Web servers and shifting network locations. Other URN systems included the Online Computer Library Center's (OCLC's) Persistent Uniform Resource Locator

(PURL)[4] server, an OSS application that works with URLs to provide a layer of abstraction between the URI and the network location of a resource, and OpenURL, which is a generic scheme for defining URIs based on a network user's rights and resource identification criteria.[5] The relationship between URLs and URNs can be seen in Figure 2.2.

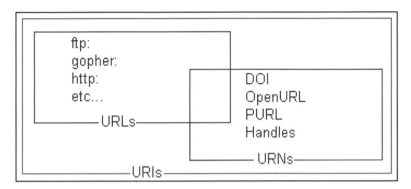

Figure 2.2. URIs are a broader concept that encompasses URLs and URNs

The HTTP daemon at the destination server machine receives the request and, after any necessary processing, a short bit of text called a *header* is passed back to the browser followed by the content. For specifying formats, the header uses an Internet standard called Multipurpose Internet Mail Extensions (MIME),[6] which, as the name implies, is used in mail systems to indicate the type of content contained in the messages received. MIME covers almost every conceivable file type and can be extended for adding unique types. Some of the most common MIME types are used for HTML (text/html) and certain types of images (image/jpg).

To see how this works in practice, imagine typing the following in your Web browser's Open or Open URL window:

```
http://www.digitallibrary.org/collections/patrick.html
```

This is a very familiar activity to most Web users. The browser sees from the URL that is an HTTP request and that it is to go to the machine with the address www.digitallibrary.org. It opens an HTTP connection on port 80 to the machine and sends the following:

```
GET /collections/index.html HTTP/1.0
User-Agent: Mozilla 4.0 (X; I; Linux-2.1.35i586)
Host: www.mymachine.org
Accept: image/gif, image/jpeg, */*
```

This request consists of *headers,* which tell the Web server certain information about the browser and identify the method that the requestor is using, in this case GET. HTTP has several basic methods or *verbs* that it recognizes (see Table 2.1).

Table 2.1. The Main HTTP Verbs

Verb	Purpose
GET	Retrieves requested resource.
POST	Used with HTML Forms to pass information.
HEAD	Retrieves only the HTTP response but not the resource. This is useful for checking whether a document has been modified or is still available.
PUT	Requests that resource be uploaded by the server.
DELETE	Requests that a resource be deleted by a server (rarely used/supported).

The request identifies the resource desired (/collections/index.html) and the HTTP protocol version used to make the request (1.0). *User-Agent* refers to the browser (Mozilla 4.0) and operating system (Linux) from which the request is coming. *Host* is the network location of the requestor, and *Accept* is the MIME types that will be accepted. Note that */* means that the requestor will accept any type back, but the request is telling the server upfront that it supports GIF and JPEG images.

The server, in turn, responds with the following:

```
HTTP/1.0 200 OK
Date: Mon, 04 Jan 2003 23:34:11 GMT
Server: Apache/1.3.1
Content-type: text/html
Content-length: 2042
Last-modified: Mon, 02 Jan 2003 20:10:11 GMT
<html>
<head>
<title>Welcome Message</title>
...
```

The first line specifies the version of HTTP that is used in the response, as well as a status code (200) and a human-readable version (OK). Table 2.2 gives the most common response codes; at least one, 404, is familiar to almost anyone who has traveled the Web. The response headers also contain information about the Web server software and version (Apache/1.3.1) and the MIME type of the response (text/html), as well as the number of bytes in the response (2042) and the last time the requested resource was modified.

Table 2.2. Common HTTP Response Codes

Code	Description
200	The request was fulfilled.
403	The request is for a resource that is forbidden.
404	The server has not found anything to match the request.
500	The server encountered an unexpected condition that prevented it from fulfilling the request.

HTTP is a stateless protocol. The connection to an HTTP daemon is made using a socket, which is the network equivalent to a telephone call. With a stateless protocol, the connection is made, the server responds, and the connection is immediately closed. It is similar to making a short phone call to your local library, listening to a recording describing the library's hours, and immediately hanging up. If you have another task to carry out on the phone, you make a separate phone call, even if you are phoning the same number each time.

A stateful protocol, on the other hand, is more like interacting with the library's reference desk, where you stay on the phone line until your question is answered. In network terms, a stateful protocol keeps a connection or socket open for an extended period, which is usually defined by either the application or the latency of the network connection. HTTP's stateless architecture reflects its original purpose: it is far more efficient and perfectly sensible when handing out HTML files to close a connection after the file has been delivered. As other types of applications have been implemented on top of HTTP, however, the stateless nature of the Web has required all manner of workarounds.

Retaining State Information

Perhaps the most recognized—some would even same infamous—mechanisms to deal with the stateless nature of the Web is to use *cookies*. Unlike the gastronomic treats most of us enjoy, cookies are used in a Web browser to record *state* information about a session. The most common example is for cookies to track a list of items in a customer's online shopping cart for a commercial vendor; cookies also could be used for recording a user's preferred display format in a digital collection as well as many others. Cookies consist of a single line of text sent using HTTP that can consist of five fields:

```
Set-cookie: name=value;expires=date;path=path;domain=domain_name;secure
```

The name parameter is what identifies the `value` you are storing on the browser. The `expires` parameter is used to tell the browser when the cookie can be ignored. `Domain` is used to limit where the cookie is valid; for example, if domain is set to *springhill.org*, only machines with an Internet address that comes from *springhill.org*, such as *mymachine.springhill.org,* will be able to use the cookie. The *secure* parameter indicates that the cookie will be transmitted only over a special HTTP connection called Hypertext Transfer Protocol Secure (HTTPS), which is transmitted over Secure Socket Layer (SSL) and is a method of encrypting HTTP traffic so that it is harder for rogue programs to view the contents of the cookie.

The following code example shows a cookie in action. Using a field called PreferredFormat, this cookie tracks the format a user prefers for viewing images. The Web server sends the following to the browser:

```
HTTP/1.0 200 OK
Date: Mon, 04 Jan 2003 23:34:11 GMT
Server: Apache/1.3.1
Content-type: text/html
Content-length: 70
Set-cookie:PreferredFormat=JPG;expires=Tues, 05-Jan-03 12:00:00 GMT
```

Cookies must at least have the *name* and *value* parameters filled; all others are optional. Despite the suspicion of cookies many people have, cookies can only store information that users have already submitted to a Web server. This doesn't mean that cookies can't be abused, but cookies cannot seek out information on their own.

Other popular mechanisms for storing site information include stuffing parameters into a URL or using hidden fields in the HTML page. A URL retaining the preferred format might look like this:

```
http://www.digitallibrary.org/browse?PreferredFormat=JPG
```

Or, if using a Web form, there might be a section of the HTML that specifies this information through a hidden element:

```
<html>
<head>
<title>Search Digital Collections</title>
</head>
<body>
<form name="dlform" action="http://www.digitallibrary.org/browse.cgi"
method="POST">
<div align="center">
```

```
Enter your query here:
<input type="text" name="Query" size="50">
<input type="hidden" name="PreferredFormat" value="JPG">
<br><br>
</div>
<input type="submit" value="Search">
</form>
</body>
</html>
```

When the user presses the Submit button (which is labeled *Search* in this example), the browser sends the values specified by the user for Query and the value specified for PreferredFormat to the server. Note that users will not see the PreferredFormat value in this case unless they utilize a "reveal source" function on the browser.

As applications that normally focus on supporting Web-based information retrieval, digital libraries are greatly impacted by HTTP and the stateless nature of the Web, and it is important to have an appreciation of the mechanisms available for retaining state information, particularly if the interface requires such functionality as retaining user preferences or supporting personalization features.

The Ubiquitous Nature of HTTP

The apparent simplicity of HTTP is deceptive. The request/response dialogue doesn't lock HTTP into one purpose, and it easily can be manipulated by other systems. Some of these systems have become well-established components of the Internet's infrastructure. For example:

- Firewalls are used to monitor network traffic and block traffic based on port numbers and other criteria.

- Caching servers temporarily store MIME content and pass it back if it can save a trip to a remote server on a subsequent request.

- Proxies act as an HTTP client to a remote service and are used to contain a browser's traffic on a specific network for IP authentication and other uses where the network interaction with a remote service must originate at a specific source.

HTTP's ability to be plugged into many different types of technologies is shown in Figure 2.3. Most Web users are unaware of how many hoops the content delivered to their browsers has been through. With the use of a *gateway,* HTTP also can be the basis for interacting with many other types of protocols.

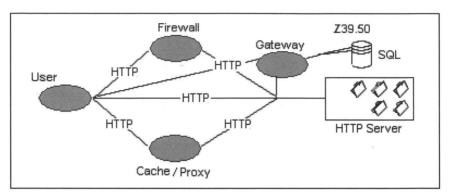

Figure 2.3. HTTP travels everywhere on the network, and there are
numerous intermediate technologies that step in along the way.

A gateway takes the results of one protocol and translates them to fit the requirements of a different protocol or application; for example, taking the results of an HTML form and using the values to formulate a query to a remote database. This is normally done with Common Gateway Interface (CGI), a specification introduced in 1994 to allow HTML content to be created dynamically. The CGI specification allows external applications to be wired into the Web as shown in Figure 2.4.

CGI programs make using the Web an interactive experience, and, just as important, they opened the door to plugging in applications that predated the Web.

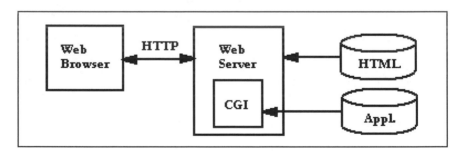

Figure 2.4. A Web server uses a CGI program to talk to an application.

In many ways, the ubiquitous nature of HTTP is a testimony to both its simplicity and extensibility. A more complex protocol would be harder to map to other applications, but HTTP represents a low-barrier means for putting applications on the Web and is flexible enough to be used in many different contexts. As a result, HTTP became firmly entrenched in the toolkits of application developers at an early stage of the Web's development and remains there today.

OSS HTTP Software: Apache

In 1991, the first HTTP server was released to the public from the European Organisation for Nuclear Research (CERN). Tim Berners-Lee, a researcher at CERN at the time, had written a proposal called *HyperText and CERN* in 1989, and it included the first definitions of HTML and HTTP.[7] Although CERN's distribution was the first HTTP server, a much more powerful version was developed by Rob McCool at the National Center for Supercomputing Applications (NCSA), University of Illinois, Urbana-Champaign. By mid-1994, McCool had left NCSA, and development of the server was stalled. Many Webmasters began developing their own extensions and bug fixes, and the development community soon realized that it needed a way to share this work. A small group of Webmasters began to plan a method of coordinating changes and updates, and they formed a collective called the Apache Group.

The first official public release (0.6.2) of the Apache Server came in April 1995, and by the end of that year, most of the original code base had been revamped and the best of the extensions had been incorporated to become version 1.0, which was released on December 1, 1995. Netcraft, the world's leading tracker of Web servers, quickly recorded that the Apache Server passed NCSA's system as the number one server on the Internet, and it remains the most popular Web server today.[8]

The Apache Group formed the Apache Software Foundation in 1999 to provide "organizational, legal, and financial support for the Apache HTTP Server." Perhaps the best description of the purpose of Apache comes from the Apache About page:

> Apache exists to provide a robust and commercial-grade reference implementation of the HTTP protocol. It must remain a platform upon which individuals and institutions can build reliable systems, both for experimental purposes and for mission-critical purposes. We believe the tools of online publishing should be in the hands of everyone, and software companies should make their money providing value-added services such as specialized modules and support, amongst other things. We realize that it is often seen as an economic advantage for one company to "own" a market—in the software industry that means to control tightly a particular conduit such that all others must pay. This is typically done by "owning" the protocols through which companies conduct business, at the expense of all those other companies. To the extent that the protocols of the World Wide Web remain "unowned" by a single company, the Web will remain a level playing field for companies large and small. Thus, "ownership" of the protocol must be prevented, and the existence of a robust reference implementation of the protocol, available absolutely for free to all companies, is a tremendously good thing.[9]

The HTTP server is the flagship application of the Apache Foundation and is continually being enhanced by both individuals and large organizations such as IBM. If ever there was an OSS success story and an example of where OSS can provide a compelling solution, Apache is it.

OSS HTTP Software: AOLServer

Apache dominates the Web server world so convincingly that you may wonder if it is even necessary to consider another option. Two reasons to consider others might be that Apache is not performing well on weak hardware for very busy sites or that Apache is deemed too complex for organizations to manage. AOLServer has its roots in a system called NaviServer, which offered a complete Web-publishing system as early as 1994. Two years later, America Online (AOL) bought AOLServer to provide the backbone of its Web presence, and by 1999, AOL had decided that it should open source AOLServer for the mutual benefit of AOL members and the public at large.[10]

AOLServer does not have the mind share and backing of Apache, but it does reflect the needs of one of the world's highest-volume Web publishers. AOLServer is extremely efficient, straightforward to install and administer, and has some great scripting tools. Unfortunately, AOL has abandoned the publishing-side tools that used AOLServer to provide a seamless system, but this server is still an attractive option for a site that is looking for a quick on-ramp to establishing a Web presence for a digital collection.

OAI-PMH

The Open Archives Initiative Protocol for Metadata Harvesting (OAI-PMH) has been called the "HTTP of digital libraries,"[11] even though the protocol actually uses HTTP as a transport mechanism between digital collections. OAI-PMH is several years younger than HTTP, with origins in a 1999 meeting in Santa Fe, New Mexico, to address a series of problems that were occurring in the e-print server world (*e-prints* are electronic versions of materials that are typically scholarly papers of a research nature). As disciplinary e-print servers became more common, it was difficult to support searching across multiple repositories.[12] Repositories needed greater capabilities to automatically identify and copy papers that had been deposited in other repositories.

The solution arrived at in Santa Fe was the definition of an interface to permit an e-print server to expose metadata for the papers it held. This would allow the metadata to be picked up by programs on the Web called *harvesters*. Harvesting programs travel around a network gathering, or harvesting, content by copying it to a central site. OAI-PMH shares with HTTP a certain simplicity. Like HTTP, OAI-PMH consists of simple *verbs* that specify conditions such as locating just the metadata that has been added or modified since a certain date (most likely based on the last time the site was harvested). The entire list of verbs is given in Table 2.3.

Table 2.3. Open Archives Initiative Protocol for Metadata Harvesting (OAI-PMH) Verbs

Verb	Purpose
Identify	Requests general information about the site
ListMetadataFormats	Retrieves the supported metadata schemes and their namespaces
ListSets	Retrieves information on the names and descriptions for groups of records (called *sets*) that can be requested; for example, "All" with a description of "All Records"
GetRecord	Returns the metadata for a single identifier
autoListIdentifiers	Requests a list of all unique identifiers; can be based on date and/or set name
ListRecords	Requests metadata for multiple records; can be based on date and/or set name

OAI-PMH divides the world into data providers (entities that respond to the OAI-PMH verbs) and service providers (entities that harvest the metadata by issuing the OAI-PMH verbs). The concept is that service providers add value to the data they harvest by defining search engines and other applications (see Figure 2.5).

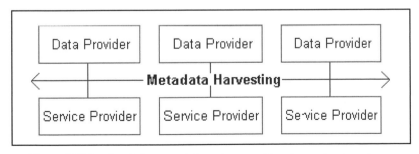

Figure 2.5 Metadata is harvested from data providers to construct services.

Although other metadata schemes can be specified, OAI-PMH mandates that Dublin Core be available. OAI is purposely designed to be "low barrier" to developers. Relatively simple criteria are used for harvesting: basically, date stamps, which identify when resources have last been modified, and sets, which group together records based on criteria defined by the data provider. There are more than 100 registered OAI-PMH data providers, and several extensions have been suggested to increase its utility to digital libraries.[13]

OSS OAI Software: Complete Systems

There are many OAI tools available. Table 2.4 lists complete systems that can be used to develop an OAI system while supplying storage and management functions. For the network location of these and other OAI systems, see the OAI section in Further Resources.

Table 2.4. Open Archives Initiative (OAI) Systems

Tool	Implementer	Type	Description
DSpace	HP Labs and MIT Libraries	Data provider	DSpace is described as a digital asset management software platform that enables institutions to easily archive digital objects. Released under MIT License.
eprints.org	University of Southampton	Data provider	This is software to run centralized, discipline-based as well as distributed, institution-based archives of scholarly publications. GPL license.
XMLFile	Virginia Tech	Data provider	This tool exposes a set of XML files in a directory as an OAI data provider.
Kepler	Old Dominion University	Data provider	Kepler is a simple and straightforward system to expose documents through OAI. Like XMLFile, Kepler is a good option if you have a set of stand-alone documents in your collection.
Arc	Old Dominion University	Service provider	A powerful harvesting system for bringing together OAI resources, Arc provides a way of bringing together and customizing disparate digital collections. Released under the NCSA license.
my.OAI		Service provider	This tool is a simple but effective harvesting system.

Z39.50

Z39.50 is the old-timer among HTTP and OAI, having roots that stretch back to the early 1970s and the Linked Systems Project for searching bibliographic databases and transferring records among the Library of Congress, the Online Computer Library Center (OCLC), the Research Libraries Group (RLG), and the Washington (now Western) Library Network (WLN). Z39.50 is a stateful protocol that allows a client machine (called an *origin*) to search a server machine (called a *target*). Despite its close association with the library community, Z39.50 is a relatively generic protocol with a rich set of functions for search and retrieval, including the ability to sort result sets and registries of objects such as *attribute sets* that specify search points. These search points can be mapped onto the indexes and search capabilities of the underlying server. Perhaps the best-known attribute set is Bib-1, originally designed for bibliographic resources but now commonly used for a wide range of applications.

Bib-1 comprises groupings of attributes, or attribute types, that define a deep level of precision in putting together queries. For example, the Use attribute defines the access point (such as *title* or *subject*), while the Relation attribute defines the relation (such as *equal to* or *greater than*) of the search term to the values in the database. These attributes correspond to numbers in the standard that Z39.50-compliant systems can use to deconstruct queries. A search might look like this in a particular interface:

```
FIND TITLE PROGRAM* OR SUBJECT UNIX
```

Here, a digital library collection contains computer science materials, and a search has been created to search for works with *program* in the title. A truncation symbol is used (*) so that the user also will see works with such titles as "Programming in Java." The collection also supports subject searching, and the term *UNIX* is used to include materials that have been designated by the collection maintainers to be about UNIX. To a Z39.50 application, however, the same search looks something like the following:

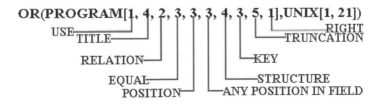

Numbers are used to specify the attributes, so that 1, which represents the attribute *Use,* is associated with the value of 4, which represents the attribute for *Title*. These attribute pairings are used within the query for as much specification as necessary to carry out the search. *Relation* (represented by the number 2) is associated with *Equal* (represented by the number 3), which normally would be the default on the server, but it is easy to imagine searches in which we might want a relation that is less than or greater than a certain term; for example, when looking at numeric data such as temperature levels recorded for scientific materials. The *Position* (3) attribute is assigned the number representing the fact that the term can be located anywhere in the field, *Structure* (4) is used to designate a keyword/*Key* (4) search, and, finally, the intent of the truncation character is captured by using the *Truncation* 5 attribute with the value for right truncation (1). Note how the subject part of the search is much simpler. Z39.50 allows for very deep precision, but there is no requirement to use the full range of precision available.

Z39.50 is more complex than either HTTP or OAI and is an important protocol for digital libraries because it is designed to meet the very real complexities of information retrieval. It also can be used as a tool to build distributed search services, also know as *federated* search systems. The client in a federated system sends a search to all of the servers comprising the federation. It can then gather the results and attempt to eliminate duplicates or perform value-added services such as clustering the results under topics, unlike the harvesting approach used with OAI that takes entire sets of records (see Figure 2.6).

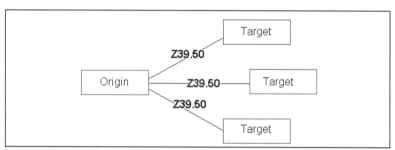

Figure 2.6. One client can search many servers using Z39.50.

There can be huge variations in the level of Z39.50 services available because of the sheer number and differing interpretations of the options in the standard. In the last few years, there has been an initiative called the Bath Profile[14] to identify a baseline set of features from the Z39.50 standard, along with a consistent approach to implementing them across servers. Conformance to the Bath Profile requires defining levels of service and is a much-needed effort to put substance into claims of Z39.50 conformance. Another Z39.50 initiative is the Search/Retrieve Web Service (SRW) protocol, which moves the decades of work in the intellectual/semantic content of Z39.50 more strongly into a Web environment.

Z39.50 Software

Z39.50 is an abstract layer on top of an existing system, so it isn't surprising that most Z39.50 tools are architected to work on top of other applications (see the Further Resources section for more information and URLs). However, there are a few open source applications that also provide the underlying database/repository system (see Table 2.5).

Table 2.5. Z39.50 Systems and Toolkits

Server	License	Description
Cheshire II	Custom	Originally designed to bring probabilistic full-text searching techniques to conventional library catalogues, Cheshire II is used to provide production searching services for a number of high-profile collections, including the Resource Discovery Network[15] built for learning institutions in the United Kingdom. The system supports both SGML and XML documents, in addition to text documents and HTML, and has sophisticated support for defining sections of SGML/XML documents for use as stand-alone content.
Isite	Custom	The Center for Networked Information Discovery and Retrieval (CNIDR) was one of the first organizations to publicly make Z39.50 software available, and Isite has roots that predate the Web. Like Zebra (see following), Isite works with an existing set of files and includes a powerful Z39.50 gateway that is used by the Library of Congress[16] among others to provide access to Z39.50 resources.
JAFER	LGPL	Java Access for Electronic Resources (JAFER) is an XML-based toolkit for adding Z39.50 support to an XML view of the collection. This is particularly useful for systems such as Cocoon, as discussed in Chapter 9, where XML is used as a conduit for tying systems together.
Zebra	GPL	Zebra is a very mature and full-featured Z39.50 implementation that allows you to immediately put a Z39.50 layer over a collection of stand-alone XML files, much like what XMLFile provides for OAI.
Z39.50/PRISE 2.0	Custom	This is a well-designed system that is available only for Solaris at the time of this writing.

Other Protocols for DLs

This section introduces protocols that later chapters examine in more depth. These protocols are supported widely outside of the digital library community; numerous open source software options for implementing them are available and can be found using the information in the Further Resources section.

SOAP

Simple Object Access Protocol (SOAP) combines XML with HTTP for accessing services, objects, and servers. It is a lynchpin of a suite of technologies called *Web Services* that leverages the Web for delivering application functions in a well-defined manner. We discuss Web services in more detail in Chapter 9, but SOAP is important because it defines a formal structure for specifying information that can be passed to a Web application, and the same structure can be used to pass the results of the request back. This structure is called an *envelope* and contains a mechanism called a *header,* which specifies rules about processing the request, and a *body,* which is the XML representation of the information that the Web application will be handed (see Figure 2.7).

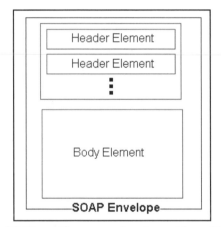

Figure 2.7. SOAP specifies an envelope to contain multiple sections.

SOAP allows a great deal of information to be passed to an application, and it leverages XML for laying out the data that goes between DL applications. Whether this extra syntax is required really depends on the application. For example, if a digital library requires requests or material served to clients to contain a digital signature, or if a request involves a complex data structure such as a list of authors and time periods for their writings, SOAP is better suited to handle such complexity than straight HTML requests.It includes facilities for *faults,* so that when things go wrong, there are options to consistently deal with application or network problems.

RSS

RDF Site Summary (RSS) is an XML-based format that allows simultaneous publication, or *syndication,* of lists of hyperlinks, along with other information or metadata, that help viewers decide whether they want to follow a link. A Web application makes use of RSS by making a *feed* or *channel* available, which consists of an XML file that shows the most recent items to be described. This normally is picked up by an *aggregator,* a program that manages a number of lists and presents them in a single interface. A simple RSS file is shown here.

```
<?xml version="1.0" ?>
<rdf:RDF
   xmlns:rdf="http://www.w3.org/1999/02/22-rdf-syntax-ns#"
   xmlns="http://purl.org/rss/1.0/">

<channel>
        <title>Digital Library News</title>
        <link>http://dl.somewhere.org/additions/</link>
        <description>New Additions to the Collection.</description>
        <language>en-us</language>
        <items>
            <rdf:Seq>
                <rdf:li resource="Ken Smith's Diaries Updated"/>
                <rdf:li resource="Smith's Original Manuscript"/>
            </rdf:Seq>
        </items>
</channel>
<item rdf:about="http://dl.somewhere.org/additions/smith/diaries/">
        <title>Ken Smith's Diaries Updated</title>
        <link>http://dl.somewhere.org/additions/smith/diaries/</link>
        < description>Ken Smith's diaries from the 1850s.</description>
</item>
<item rdf:about="http://dl.somewhere.org/additions/smith/orig/">
        <title>Smith's Original Manuscript</title>
        <link>http://dl.somewhere.org/additio ns/smith/orig/</link>
        <description>A scanned imaged of Ken Smith's original
        manuscript.</description>
</item>
</rdf:RDF>
```

If this file is installed on a Web server, the address can be fed into an aggregator and the results typically will resemble those shown in Figure 2.8.

As the RSS file is updated, the aggregator continues to return to the site and highlight changes. RSS may seem like an odd choice in this list, but content syndication is an important method of delivering content to portals and other third-party systems, and it is a solid option for distributing information concerning a digital collection or news from the organization itself. HubMed,[17] for example, uses RSS to disseminate updates for specific medical literature queries.

Figure 2.8 AmphetaDesk,[18] an open source RSS aggregator,
is used to track headlines from a number of sources.

Shibboleth

Shibboleth is an authentication and authorization project under the auspices of Internet 2, a consortium of over 190 universities working in partnership with nearly 100 industry vendors and government agencies to develop and deploy advanced network applications and technologies. *Authentication* refers to establishing a digital identity for a user, such as "Jane Smith." *Authorization* is the process that establishes which resources are associated with a digital identity; for example, Jane Smith may be a faculty member at a certain university and may have rights to licensed resources because of this affiliation.

The technology provided by Shibboleth operates at a layer between the user and the desired resource. Like Z39.50, Shibboleth uses the notion of an *origin* and *target*. When a user first attempts to access a resource protected by Shibboleth, Shibboleth redirects the user to an authentication service at the origin site. Shibboleth does not perform the authentication; instead, it generates a temporary reference to a user if authentication is granted by the local system and passes the reference to the remote resource's system. The remote system then uses the reference to check with Shibboleth about levels of authorization or attributes to determine whether the user has access to the resource (see Figure 2.9). The attributes are drawn from another Internet 2 initiative called eduPerson, a project to identify a common set of attributes for education, such as "affiliation."

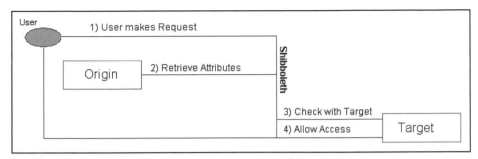

Figure 2.9. Shibboleth assembles attributes before checking with the target system. If the attributes are acceptable, the user is given access to the resource.

Shibboleth is a mature technology, especially compared to the existing authentication/authorization schemes commonly in place for library systems. Many digital resources currently utilize IP authentication in which a user's network address is used as the basis for accessing resources, an approach that allows proxies and other mechanisms to gain access by using their own IP addresses. The drawback is that IP authentication is fairly easy to bypass. Shibboleth is much more granular and provides better security for resources. Perhaps the most important aspect of Shibboleth for digital libraries is that it provides controls to protect privacy and online identity. This is a looming issue for digital libraries and is currently a high-profile topic for their physical counterparts.[19]

Putting It All Together

Protocols make network systems work together and are the basis of many formal communications. Digital libraries depend on protocols, particularly HTTP, OAI-PHM, and Z39.50, to provide services. Think of HTTP as the highway between digital libraries, with OAI as a friendly but comprehensive census taker that periodically turns up on the highway for updates on changes in the collection, and Z39.50 as a sometimes more demanding visitor asking for less predicable and more specific information on the collection. SOAP, RSS, and Shibboleth promise to enhance further and expand the boundaries of digital library services.

3 OSS Authoring Tools for Digital Libraries

Content is at the heart of all collections, digital or otherwise; in digital libraries the content manifests itself in multiple ways. It often must be created from a physical object and must have the capability to be rendered in multiple formats and media. The open source software world is rich in authoring tools for digital collections. *Authoring,* in this sense, refers to the creation of the digital version of the object; for example, creating images of pages of a rare manuscript. Some might argue that this is a peculiar type of authorship, but generally, its foremost purpose is to service the content of the original author(s) and render the information into digital format.

Image Tools

As noted in Chapter 1, images are a frequent building block of digital collections. Image formats generally are either bitmap graphics (also called raster graphics), which are collections of dots (pixels) that fit together to make up an image, or vector graphics, which use lines instead of dots to describe images, which can result in dramatically smaller files sizes. Some examples of bitmap file formats include PNG, GIF, JPEG/JPG, BMP, XBM, and TIFF (see the glossary for definitions). Examples of popular vector graphic formats include AI and EPS. Vector file formats normally are used in digital libraries only when images are created from scratch. Bitmap file formats are considered better choices for such material as photographs and screenshots in which color and shading can vary greatly.

Color depth and compression are also important considerations in selecting image formats. *Color depth* refers to the range of colors available for each dot or pixel in an image; for example, 8-bit color supports 256 colors for each pixel. Compression is either *lossless,* in which all of the information in the original bitmap is retained, or *lossy,* in which some information (such as color shifts) is discarded to achieve a smaller file size. Some formats, such as PNG, support *transparency,* which allows you to replace the background color of an image to remove distracting details and concentrate focus on the main part of the graphic.

Given the variety of image formats and possible combinations for compression and color depth, it is not surprising that very few tools are considered capable of handling the level of editing required for digital libraries. This also might be one of the few areas in the digital library world in which debates over tools have resulted in wide consensus. For commercial packages, the flagship image tool for digital libraries is Adobe Photoshop,[1] a full-featured and powerful image-editing system. Many organizations that do extensive work with images already have experience with Photoshop. Although licensing for commercial image-editing products can be expensive, it may turn out to be cheaper than the server and server-side infrastructure necessary for maintaining a digital collection. In other words, money spent on client-side authoring tools may be money well spent.

The good news is that a reasonable OSS alternative to Photoshop has emerged: the GNU Image Manipulation Program, or the GIMP (see Figure 3.1). If you haven't already committed to Photoshop, the GIMP is a viable alternative. Some of the GIMP's features include a rich suite of painting tools, including different types of brushes, support for images of any size, and a mechanism called Perl-Gimp for calling internal GIMP functions from external programs.

Figure 3.1. The GIMP in action on a Macintosh.

The GIMP's functionality makes it ideal for batch processing and incorporating into other programs. For example, Gallery Maker is a batch conversion process built using Perl-Gimp that generates an HTML thumbnail gallery from a directory of images (see Figure 3.2).

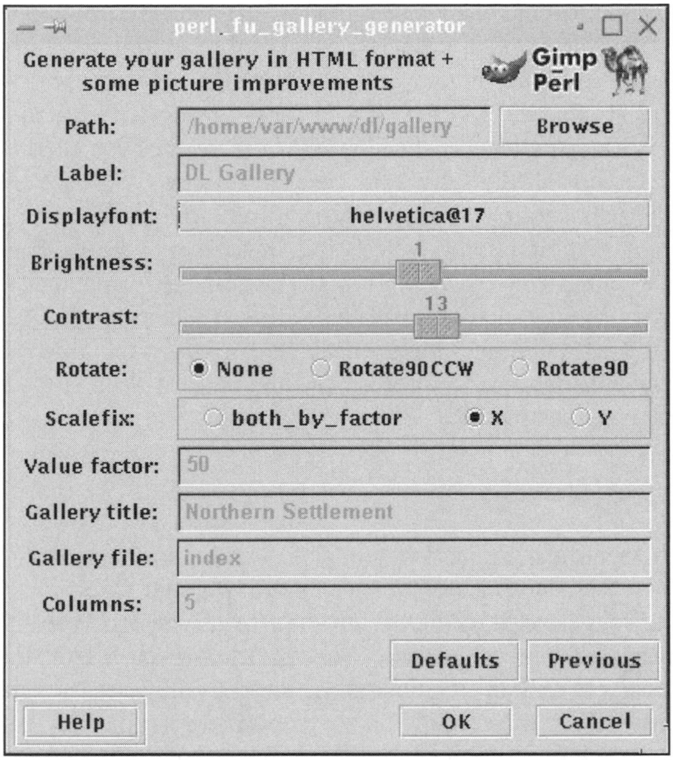

Figure 3.2. One of many examples of the power of Perl-Gimp.

One of the most important features of the GIMP is that it supports Adobe's proprietary PSD format, the native bitmap file format for Photoshop, as well as Filter Factory format, which is a Photoshop file format for creating galleries. This not only allows you to easily switch from Photoshop to the GIMP (or vice versa), but also opens the door to the many Photoshop resources available on the Web. The GIMP is available for all major platforms and is published under a GPL license.

For digitization projects, one of the most essential capabilities of graphics tools is the ability to handle large TIFF (Tagged Image File Format) files, a format originally developed by Aldus Corporation to save images created by scanners, frame grabbers, and photo-editing programs. This format has been widely accepted and supported as an image transfer format not tied to specific software or hardware. There are many factors in selecting scanning and digital formats, but, generally speaking, image materials that are the result of scanning or that are created from scratch should be at a resolution of 400 to 600 dpi (dots per inch, a term used interchangeably with ppi, which stands for pixels per inch) and in 24-bit color (in which each dot is capable of displaying up to 16.8 million gradations of red/green/blue color) to qualify as an archival *master*, loosely defined as capturing content in as high a quality as is reasonably possible.

Some of the resources identified in the Further Resources section give detailed information on image formats and scanning guidelines, but suffice it to say that images in digital library collections almost always involve huge files and intensive graphic capabilities. If you are working with the materials to be housed in the digital collection, then the GIMP is the tool you need to handle this task. However, not all digital library image activities must involve high-end tools like Photoshop and the GIMP. For example, images may be needed to entice users into the digital library's Web site, or there may be TIFF archival masters that have been used to create files in another image format that, in turn, need to be edited for Internet delivery. Table 3.1 lists a selection of OSS image tools that might be useful in digital library projects for which the GIMP is too elaborate (for more information on the applications and for Web site addresses, see the Further Resources section).

Other Media

Objects in a digital collection conceivably can require media editors of every type. Table 3.2 shows a selection of several popular OSS options for working with non-image-based media (for more information and Web site addresses, see the Further Resources section). For the most part, digital libraries have tended to consist of textual and illustrated materials, but there is a growing trend toward multimedia collections with the increasing availability of cheap disk storage and a growing amount of content authored solely in these media. Multimedia applications have long been considered an area in which OSS trails behind commercial applications, but the gap is closing.

Table 3.1. Open Source Software Image Tools

Application	Platform	Notes	License
ImageMagick	Linux, most other variants of UNIX, Windows, Macintosh	A full-featured editing package, not quite up to the GIMP in functionality, but possibly the strongest for using from programming environments.	Available under a BSD-style license.
OpenOffice Draw	Linux, Solaris, Windows, Macintosh (OS X in beta)	Basic, but well-designed graphic tool.	OpenOffice.org uses a variety of licenses for the source code, including the GNU General Public License (GPL) and the Sun Industry Standards Source License.
GNU Paint	Linux–GNOME	Much more basic than the GIMP, but a very nice option for light editing if you use a GNOME desktop in Linux.	GPL
SANE (Scanner Access Now Easy)	Linux, most variants of Unix, Mac OS X	Similar to TWAIN (jokingly referred to as a "Technology Without An Interesting Name," though the acronym originates from the saying, "never the twain shall meet"), but much more focused on UNIX. SANE is a key technology in using image-capturing devices such as scanners with Linux and is usually part of an application. For example, xscanimage[2] is a front end to SANE that works with the GIMP and supports Mustek and Hewlett-Packard (HP) flatbed scanners.	GPL

Table 3.2. Open System Software Applications for Non-Image-Based Media

Application	Media Type	Platform	Notes	License
Bender	Three-dimensional (3D) graphics	Linux, most variants of Unix, Mac OS X, Windows	Bender has been around for several years and is a solid 3D modeling tool.	GPL
Cinelerra LiVES	Video creation and editing	Linux (where such tools are rare)	Much needed options for Linux desktops.	GPL
Sweep SoX	Sound editing and mixing	Linux, BeOS (a platform often used for multimedia work)	Sweep has a friendly interface, while SoX packs a lot of power into the command line.	GPL
Mr. Project	Project management	Linux – GNOME Desktop	Not a media editor per se, but a class of software that is invaluable for media conversion projects and still extremely rare in the OSS world.	GPL

XML Editors

At least one XML editor calls itself "not another XML-tree editor,"[3] and this description gets to the root of XML editing. Many editors faithfully reflect the structure of XML documents, the "tree" in the description, and a common XML editing layout is shown in Figure 3.3. At the same time, most word processors have started to support XML content creation directly so that the experience of creating XML is very similar to working with general documents.

Which is preferable? It really depends on the content and even on the preferences of the person doing the typing. In general, a word processing approach works better for projects for which an intimate knowledge of the XML structure is not required. Perhaps one day software designers faced with alternatives like these will automatically provide both and allow the user the option. It is rare indeed that one alternative will suffice for *every* need.

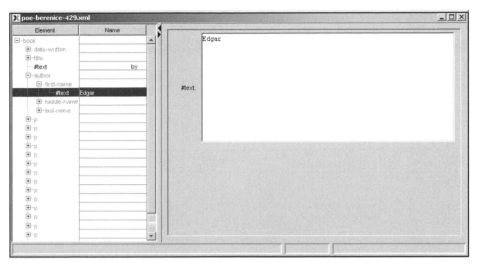

Figure 3.3. Pollo displays the XML tree of the document.

Another key decision concerns validation, the process by which a DTD or Schema is used to check a document's format. Some editing applications have extensions that support XML, but they do not validate the results. This might not be as problematic as it first seems since much of the content might be text based and does not require rigorous checking at the time of creation. In some projects, it may even be preferable to validate after the bulk of data entry is complete.

On the other hand, validation can catch problems at the time of content creation and before it is moved to a database or shared with other sites. A few XML editing tools also have support for creating stylesheets, which we look at more closely in Chapter 4. Stylesheets can be very useful if the content is presented in many different formats and the content creator is the one designing the presentation.

Many XML tools are written in Java and require a Java environment in order to run. Java is a platform-independent programming language from Sun Microsystems that is currently the most taught language in universities and is a commonly available environment in many organizations. Java is particularly well suited for XML applications because it means the resulting application can be deployed on almost any major operating system, hence the Java slogan "write once, run anywhere."[4]

Despite the goal of providing seamless solutions on any platform, Java-based systems can involve configuration issues. Java applications are designed to run in the Java Virtual Machine (JVM), a software-based "machine" that sits on top of a computer's operating system and interfaces with the software environment installed. JVMs can indeed be obtained easily for most popular operating systems, but Java applications often have dependencies on other Java programs that are not part of the standard JVM installation. For the most part, setting up a JVM is simply a matter of running an installation program; all of the Java-based tools listed in the Table 3.3 are fairly straightforward to get running.

Table 3.3. Extensible Markup Language (XML) Authoring Tools

Application	Type	Platforms	Notes	Validating	XSL Support	License
Amaya	Tree	Linux, most variants of UNIX, Mac OS X, Windows	This editor is made available by the W3C and, not surprisingly, shines for standards support. As a general Web editor, Amaya has fierce competition but has unique support for MathML[5] and annotation features, as well as some support for RDF.	DTD	Not yet, some cascading style sheets (CSS) support	W3C Software License
Pollo	Tree	Java-based, all major platforms	Very functional and clean application for XML editing.	DTD and XML Schema	No	MIT
Xerlin	Tree	Java-based, all major platforms	A rapidly evolving application, well-designed interface.	DTD	No	Apache
KOffice	Word processor	Linux, with Windows coming	Like OpenOffice, KOffice uses XML as a native format.	No	No	GPL
OpenOffice Writer	Word processor	Linux, most variants of UNIX, Mac OS X, Windows	XML is a native and documented format.	Only in terms of its own DTD	No	GPL
Cooktop	Tree	Windows only	Very sleek XML tool for Windows desktops.	DTD	Yes	Binary is freeware, no access to source
Jedit	Tree	Java-based, all major platforms	General-purpose and high-quality text editor, supports XML and Extensible Stylesheet Language (XSL) through plug-ins. One of the author's favorite editors.	DTD	Yes	GPL

Table 3.3 lists some of the most popular OSS editors that support XML (for more information on the applications, see the Further Resources section); however, this is a moving target since so many applications are being fitted with XML capabilities.

Up Close: OpenOffice

In 2000, at an open source conference in Monterey, California, Sun announced its plans to release the source code for its Star Office suite as an OSS distribution. The result was OpenOffice,[6] possibly considered the leading challenger to the Microsoft Office suite. OpenOffice is of interest from an OSS perspective for many reasons, not the least of which is its XML-centric file structure.

When you save your work in any of the applications in the OpenOffice suite, the data are placed in a compressed, or *zipped,* archive that contains several XML and other files describing the content. For example, saving this chapter in OpenOffice Writer results in an archive called testing.sxw, which contains the files shown in Figure 3.4. These files are described in Table 3.4.

```
arhyno@pyman /tmp$ unzip -l testing.sxw
Archive: testing.sxw
   Length     Date      Time     Name
 ------------  -----    ------    ------
     1765    03-06-03   21:13    content.xml
     4603    03-06-03   21:13    styles.xml
     1179    03-06-03   21:13    meta.xml
     5504    03-06-03   21:13    settings.xml
      752    03-06-03   21:13    META-INF/manifest.xml
 ------------          ----------
   13803                 5 files
```

Figure 3.4. A listing of the content of an OpenOffice Writer archive.

It is important to realize that the OpenOffice DTDs are not included in the archive and can be found either in the share directory of the OpenOffice installation (for example, /usr/lib/openoffice/share/dtd/ in Linux/UNIX and \Program Files\OpenOffice\share in Windows) or at the OpenOffice Web site. If you use a general XML editing tool for documents created with OpenOffice, you must have access to these to use validation features in the XML application.

The use of an open, documented XML format is of interest in itself for archiving and preserving the contents of documents, but it also provides a way to leverage OpenOffice as an editing tool for a digital library project that follows a particular DTD or Schema. You can use OpenOffice's template and style features to tighten the control of the content produced in Writer, and you also can convert documents produced in other word processing packages into OpenOffice format to reformat them as open XML files, so that you can modify or augment the XML that is produced.

Putting It All Together

There are open source tools for almost every conceivable type of content found in digital libraries. XML editing tools are likely to be of particular interest in digital library projects, and both tree-based and word processor–based applications are available. OpenOffice is a strong option for XML content since it provides a worthy alternative to commercial office suites. Although OpenOffice lacks some of the functionality of the Microsoft Office suite, it is suitable for meeting the bulk of most organizations' needs. The quality of OSS tools today is at a point where a digital library project, even one involving extensive digitization and image manipulation, can be carried out completely with open source software.

Table 3.4. The Open Office Archive Structure

File	Purpose
content.xml	Contains the main document content.
styles.xml	Contains any styles that are used in the document. Note that these are not the same as XML stylesheets. This file is comparable to CSS or XSL-Formatting Objects (XSL-FO), as covered in chapter 4, and contains information on font sizes and other presentation elements.
meta.xml	Loosely based on Dublin Core, this file contains information describing the document, such as the author name.
settings.xml	This file contains the document and view settings (such as magnification level and selected printer) that are typically specific to your environment.
Pictures	This directory contains any images (in their native, binary formats) that are used in the document. In the example in Figure 3.4, there are no images in the document, so this directory is not created.
META-INF/ manifest.xml	This file provides additional information about the files in the archive, such as MIME types.

OSS Tools for Manipulating and Transforming XML

4

In Chapter 1, we looked at some of the advantages of using XML in digital libraries and specifically identified its importance for opening the door to other technologies. One of the richest technologies that XML enables is called *trans-formations*. As the name implies, a transformation takes content in one format and reproduces it in another. The technology that enables transformations for XML is called the Extensible Stylesheet Language for Transformations (XSLT), and it is one of the shortest paths to realizing the value of using XML for digital content.

XSLT and XSLT Processors

XSLT is used to deliver XML content to external applications, such as Web browsers, using a mechanism called *stylesheets*. Programs that work with XSLT are called *processors*, and they empower stylesheets to deliver presentation and transformation capabilities to XML content. Stylesheets have roots in SGML and entered the Web in 1996 when the W3C introduced a standard called cascading style sheets (CSS). CSS offers Web developers precise control over layout, fonts, colors, backgrounds, and other typographical effects, as well as a way to update the appearance and formatting of an unlimited number of pages by changing just one document. For example, consider a very simple HTML file:

```
<HTML>
<HEAD>
<!-Start Stylesheet Rules ->
<STYLE TYPE="text/css">
<!-
H1 { color: green; font-size: 35px; font-family: impact }
->
</STYLE>
```

47

```
<!—End of Stylesheet Rules —>
<TITLE>Digital Collections at My Library</TITLE>
</HEAD>
<BODY>
<H1>Coming soon!</H1>
<P>We will soon be announcing that several major new collections will be
available to library users.</P>
</BODY>
</HTML>
```

CSS uses a series of directives, or *rules*, to specify how content should be displayed. The preceding rule tells the Web browser that all text surrounded by <H1></H1> should be displayed in green. Each rule consists of a selector and a declaration. In the example, H1 is the selector. It's the tag to which the style is attached. The declaration is the definition of what the style actually is. The declaration also consists of two parts, the property (in this case, color) and the value (green).

On its own, an embedded style sheet is somewhat useful. But the real advantages come when style sheets are referenced separately. This is done using the <LINK> tag. So, if we put our H1 rule in a file called Style.css, we could achieve the same effect by referencing it as shown:

```
<HTML>
<HEAD>
<LINK REL=stylesheet HREF="Style.css" TYPE="text/css">
<TITLE>Digital Collections at My Library</TITLE>
</HEAD>
<BODY>
<H1>Coming soon!</H1>
<P>We will soon be announcing several major collections will be
available to library users.</P>
</BODY>
</HTML>
```

You can link to the same style sheets file from an unlimited number of HTML or XML documents. This is important because it allows a Web author or developer to specify some stylistic conventions for a site and maintain this consistency in one place instead of having to edit each file individually. The XML syntax is similar to what is used in HTML:

```
<? xml-stylesheet type="text/css" href="Style.css" ?>
```

CSS also allows the definition of additions for special processing using a construct called *classes*. For example, if you wanted some paragraphs in your documents to be red and others to be blue, you can create two classes of P (paragraph), each with its own rules. The rules (either embedded in the document or in an external file) would look like this:

```
P.red { color: red }
P.blue { color: purple }
```

Classes don't have to be associated with any tags; for example:

```
.red { color: red }
```

In this case, the CLASS="red" directive can be used with HTML tags as needed and is not limited to the <p> tag.

The bad news is that CSS is not supported by every browser. As a general rule, you need to test your CSS creations on several browsers to ensure you are getting the desired effect on those that do support CSS, while not torpedoing any chance of working with the content for browsers that do not support it. Not only older browsers require special attention, many adaptive technologies completely ignore CSS directives. This becomes a problem if you use certain fonts to denote types of content, for example, using Garamond for quotations.

When CSS Is Not Enough

Although CSS can save considerable grief in managing the appearance of documents, there are lots of functions you may want to carry out on XML content that CSS doesn't supply. For example, you may want to change the order of elements in a document, combine multiple documents into one, or produce output that isn't remotely related to XML or HTML. In other words, you may want to do more than *ornamenting* the content of your documents, and this is where XSLT comes in.

Using XSLT, you can transform an XML document into any text-based format. Consider a very simple XML file:

```
<?xml version="1.0"?>
<decision>
The People for Stylesheets versus the Web Anarchists. The jury has sided
with  the Stylesheets for reasons of consistency and web master sanity.
</decision>
```

The file contains legal decisions from court cases, which you collect in your digital library. This content may have numerous uses, and a common one is likely to be delivering this information to Web browsers using HTML. To convert it to an HTML document, you could create an XSLT file that looks like this:

```
<?xml version="1.0"? xmlns:xsl="http://www.w3.org/1999/ XSL/Transform">
<html>
<head>
<title>List of Decisions</title>
</head>
<body>
<xsl:template match="decision">
  <p>
    <xsl:value-of/>
  </p>
```

```
</xsl:template>
</body>
</html>
```

Notice that this file uses a namespace, designated by the <xmlns> tag. A *namespace,* as explained in the discussion of RDF in Chapter 1, is a logical construct that brings together all the elements for a particular *vocabulary,* or list of possible element names and attributes for the type of XML file. This means that the XSLT processor recognizes that the *xsl* prefix in the file indicates elements associated with the Web address http://www.w3.org/1999/XSL/Transform. Namespaces become very important if elements are being used from many different types of XML content. This file tells an XSLT processor that everywhere that the <decision> tags are found, the content delimited by the tags should be printed out surrounded by <p> and </p>. The results would be as follows:

```
<html>
<head>
<title>List of Decisions</title>
</head>
<body>
<p>The People for Stylesheets versus the Web Anarchists. The jury has
sided with the  Stylesheets for reasons of consistency and web master
sanity.
</p>
</body>
</html>
```

XSLT makes extensive use of a standard called XPath,[1] a separate W3C recommendation that defines a syntax for locating and extracting any part of an XML document. The `match="decision"` expression in the preceding XSLT document relies on XPath for matching and can be a much more elaborate expression. For example, XPath could locate and pull out all the tags with a certain attribute, such as <author> tags in which an attribute called "surname" is equal to "Twain." The advantage of using an existing standard is that there are other W3C technologies, such as XPointer (a standard for linking XML content),[2] that can take advantage of the same syntax. In other words, becoming familiar with XPath and XSLT can be useful groundwork for working with other XML technologies.

XSLT documents can be specified directly in an XML file in the same manner as CSS; for example:

```
<?xml-stylesheet type="text/xsl" href="style.xsl"?>
```

In this case, the intention is that the target audience for the XML file is using an XSLT-capable browser, so the formatting takes place on the user's desktop. Internet Explorer 4 and later versions and Mozilla 6 and later versions, for example, use their own XSLT processor when handed a file with this directive. However, some browser users potentially will not have these capabilities, and client-side styling generally is frowned upon. As we see later, there are ways of taking advantage of XSLT without forcing certain browsers to be used for viewing the content.

Sorting Out XSLT

XSLT is a powerful language for transforming content, but is often a source of great confusion because the W3C working group responsible for creating an Extensible Stylesheet Language (XSL) issued two recommendations, one for transforming information (XSLT), and the XSL Recommendation called "Formatting/Flow Objects" (XSL-FO) for paginating content. However, both usually are expressed together. Moreover, to further confuse the situation, XSLT files often have an .xsl extension!

XSL-FO is a less mature standard at this point, but it also plays an important role in digital libraries because it prescribes how information is to be printed. This is important not only because users of the DL may require certain types of printing products but, the content itself may sometimes need to be reproduced to physically match the original artifact, such as broadsheets and posters. XSL-FO documents can be quite large since paginated information is often complex. For example, creating navigation tools such as page numbers, headers, and footers requires some accommodation of the constraints of the target medium. Figure 4.1 shows how all these style sheet technologies come together.

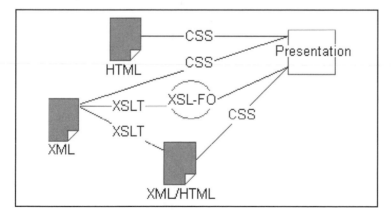

Figure 4.1. XML and style sheet relationships. Note the important role that CSS continues to play for presentation purposes.

As a general rule, if the documents in your collection don't have to be rearranged, use CSS. Otherwise, use XSLT, in one of two ways: generate the style properties together with the rearranged text, using XSL-FO for producing page-oriented content; or generate a new XML or HTML document and provide a CSS style sheet for that new document.

This is a very brief introduction to XSLT, but sufficient to allow you to appreciate why XSLT is important for XML content. The following tools are sometimes called *server-side* processors, meaning that they have no Web browser dependencies. As noted earlier, browser support for XSLT varies, and you rarely have control over which version of which browser accesses your collection. Just as important, there often may be times when the content will need to be delivered to nonbrowser systems that lack any XSLT capabilities; for example, mobile devices such as personal digital assistants (PDAs) and, yes, even physical media such as paper. Server-side processors are what frees the content of a digital library to work with the widest array of technologies and devices.

AxKit

AxKit[3] is an XML system for Apache built with mod_perl.[4] We discuss Perl more fully in Chapter 8, but you already may be aware that it is a wildly popular all-purpose scripting language. The *mod* prefix means that this version of Perl is embedded into Apache, resulting in much better performance than invoking a Perl environment separately.

AxKit comes with no less than two XSLT processors or modules. One is built around Perl's own XML::XSLT module and a much faster version from Ginger Alliance Limited called Sablotron. AxKit uses Apache's notion of handlers, in which the server detects the MIME types of files that are requested and invokes a specified program to work with the request.

In this case, Apache passes requests that have MIME type xml to AxKit, and in turn, AxKit looks for the <?xml-stylesheet?> directive (as seen in the discussion on stylesheets) and performs the transformation using the preferred XSLT processor. This is specified in Apache's Httpd.conf file:

```
SetHandler perl-script
PerlHandler AxKit
AxAddStyleMap text/xsl Apache::AxKit::Language::Sablot
```

AxKit also allows a default stylesheet to be defined in cases in which no stylesheet is specified, and it uses caching, so that it makes a user wait for a transformation only if the stylesheet or the content has been updated since the last version was put into the cache.

XSLT is just one of the functions that AxKit supplies. This application has tools for working with XML content directly from Perl scripts and support for creating XML from various data sources. These sources include relational databases, cookies, and Web form parameters, achieved through an Apache technology called Extensible Server Pages (XSP) that allows you to add extra tags to your XML to provide custom functionality.

AxKit is an excellent choice for a digital library consisting of individual XML files, especially if the organization already uses Apache. Perl runs on almost as many platforms as Apache does, and the installation is usually straightforward, especially if you have access to Perl expertise within your organization.

Cocoon

Apache Cocoon is billed as an "XML publishing framework."[5] It is a Java-based application officially supported by the Apache Foundation and is one of the most mature XML environments available in either the OSS or commercial world. Cocoon uses the Simple API for XML (SAX),[6] originally a Java-only application programming interface (API) that was the first widely adopted API for XML in Java. SAX is now available for several programming languages, and it is basically a developer's tool for talking to XML. The SAX connection is important for Cocoon, because it allows Cocoon to plug XML technologies together in a way that is very extensible.

XSLT is used through Cocoon in the same manner as almost everything else, in what the Apache Group calls *component pipelines*. The pipelines use SAX events for communication. This is a neat feature because many XML tools have to consume a large XML document before they can start doing anything useful to it. An events approach is far more efficient; for example, given this XML document:

```
<?xml version="1.0"?>
<doc>
<para>Digital Library Report is due tomorrow.</para>
</doc>
```

SAX's approach is to let the application know its progress by issuing an event as it works through the document. In this case, SAX might respond with the following:

```
"hey! I started the document"
"hey! the first element is doc"
"hey! doc element has an element called para"
"hey! para has the value 'Digital Library Report is due tomorrow.'"
"hey! I have encountered the end of the para element"
"hey! I have encountered the end of the doc element"
"hey! I have finished the document, bye for now"
```

Although these interruptions may seem like a nuisance, a computer usually can perform a significant amount of work between each request for information, and programmers tend to be very happy with event-driven technologies. These requests are passed through the pipeline through a series of components called generators, transformers, and serializers:

- The *generator* component initiates the first SAX events by acting on a request, such as a browser asking for a file, in which case it will start reading the file and start issuing events.

- The events are passed to the *transformer*. This is where the XSLT processing takes place, though any kind of transformation can be plugged in. In Cocoon, multiple transformers can be specified and "chained" so that the XML output of one becomes the input for the next.

- After the transformation(s), the response is passed back in the appropriate format. This is the task of the *serializer*. For example, it may need to set the MIME type for HTML if the request came from a browser.

The process can be seen in Figure 4.2. Cocoon ships with a number of these components, which were donated over the years by users and developers. PDFSerializer,[7] which produces a Portable Document Format (PDF) stream out of XSL-FO SAX events, and SVG2JPGSerializer,[8] which produces a JPEG stream out of the XML standard for specifying images called Scalable Vector Graphics (SVG),[9] have generated considerable interest. These components allow PDFs and JPEGs to be generated automatically from XML content.

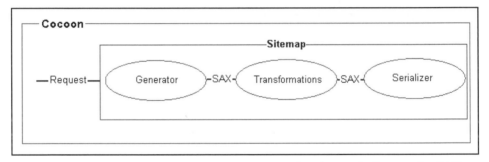

Figure 4.2. A Web request can be processed by a series of components in Cocoon using SAX.

Cocoon brings components together through a construct called a sitemap, a sort of a blueprint for telling Cocoon how to assemble components into pipelines that produce both static and dynamic resources. For example, given the following XML file:

```
<?xml version="1.0"?>
<page>
<title>Rare Manuscripts Collection</title>
<content>
<para>Welcome to the Rare Manuscripts Collection. We hope you like what
you see!</para>
</content>
</page>
```

we might use the following sitemap:

```
<map:pipeline>
<map:match pattern="Welcome.html">
<map:generate src="rare_manuscripts/Welcome.xml"/>
<map:transform src="stylesheets/Page2html.xsl"/>
<map:serialize type="html"/>
</map:match>
<map:match pattern="Welcome.wml">
<map:generate src="rare_manuscripts/Welcome.xml"/>
<map:transform src="stylesheets/Page2wml.xsl"/>
<map:serialize type="wap"/>
</map:match>
<map:match pattern="Welcome.pdf">
<map:generate src="rare_manuscripts/Welcome.xml"/>
<map:transform src="stylesheets/Page2fo.xsl"/>
<map:serialize type="fo2pdf"/>
</map:match>
</map:pipeline>
```

In this case, a Web request for Welcome.html will cause Cocoon to create an HTML version of the Welcome.xsl file by using the XSLT document called Page2html.xsl. A Wireless Application Protocol (WAP) device, such as a cell phone, that requests Welcome.wml will get a WAP version courtesy of Page2wml.xsl. Finally, a request for Welcome.pdf will use XSL-FO to produce a PDF file. In each instance, the content is contained in Welcome.xml, and there is no need to maintain three versions for different uses.

Sitemaps can be generalized to refer to more than individual files. For example:

```
<map:match pattern=" *.*">
<map:generate src="collections/{1}.xml"/>
<map:transform src=" stylesheets/page2html.xsl"/>
<map:serialize type="html"/>
</map:match>
```

Here, a request to Welcome.html will match the file Welcome.xml. This happens through what are called *wildcards,* which may be familiar to you if you have a preference for working with files from the command prompt. In this case, the {1} in the expression says, "Give me the word before the period in the request."

Another feature of sitemaps and Cocoon's component structure can be seen in the following fragment. Here, a Web browser is tested to see whether it can handle JPEG images; if it can't (meaning that it is a very dated browser), a Graphics Interchange Format (GIF) image is delivered. In this case, the image is stored in SVG format, meaning that it is an XML document and the images are created with the built-in XSLT processor. Finally, Cocoon will check its cache, and if the image recently has been produced for another browser, Cocoon will

pull it from the cache instead of going through the transformation step. This saves resources on the server and achieves better response time for the user of the browser.

```
<map:match pattern="images/dl">
<map:generate src="images/dl.svg"/>
<map:select type="browser">
<map:when test="accepts('image/jpg')">
<map:serialize type="svg2jpg"/>
</map:when>
<map:otherwise>
<map:serialize type="svg2gif"/>
</map:otherwise>
</map:select>
</map:match>
```

About Directory Structures

When working with AxKit and Cocoon or, indeed, almost any Web server, it is often the case that you will specify directories for different kinds of content. In the preceding example, the `images` directory contains graphics files related to the collection. It is well worth using directory structures to your advantage when trying to organize a digital collection that consists of individual files. For example, the Barren Lands project[10] at the University of Toronto uses directory names to identify different types of documents, such as letters and diaries. Letters are numbered sequentially; for instance, a two-page letter from the explorer Joseph Tyrrell can be stored as follows:

```
tyrrell/letters/L1001/0001
tyrrell/letters/L1001/0002
```

Whenever you are working with directories, it is a good idea to lay out the structure in a manner that makes it easy to recognize where certain classes of content may be stored. Like the file folders in the nearest file cabinet, the effort it takes to arrange the folders will pay dividends when it comes time to retrieve material. For many small to medium-sized collections, a logical directory system in combination with a Web-publishing system such as AxKit or Cocoon may suffice to create a flexible digital library. Later, we discuss several database options for storing digital collections, but don't underestimate what a well-designed directory structure can accomplish.

Putting It All Together

XML can be transformed by XSLT processors. By storing content in XML, CSS and XSLT stylesheets provide the ability to produce the formats and media that your user community desires, while retaining a useful separation between how your content is stored and how it is presented. Digital libraries one day may be the primary publishers of information for organizations, storing content in both digital and analog formats. The ability to repurpose content without having to rework it is an important step toward making digital libraries an integral part of the knowledge cycle. XSLT is an important technology for digital libraries, and, as we discuss in Chapter 9, stylesheets are an essential tool for tying different Web-based technologies together. We have just skimmed the surface here, but this is enough to get you started using XSLT tools.

5 Open Source Relational Databases for Digital Libraries

Relational databases, or relational database management systems (RDBMSs), date back to 1970 with work carried out by E. F. Codd at IBM.[1] At that time, IBM was introducing new mainframe computers and was looking for flexible approaches to storing data. After all, why would customers buy bigger hardware unless it could do a lot more with their data?

The solution Codd proposed was to store data in tables. In Codd's model (see Figure 5.1), columns typically represent the categories of the data; for example, address or phone number. The *row* is a unique instance of the data, such as "123 Library Lane," and the *field* is the value of the category for each row.

			COLUMN Address
			↓
ROW →			FIELD 123 Library Lane

Figure 5.1. Relational database tables contain columns, rows, and fields.

Before relational databases, data was stored in formats that could be very complex and often required custom programming to retrieve individual values or modify them. Something as simple as changing a telephone number might require a programmer to deal with special constructs just to reach where this value was stored. A table structure was a much easier way of defining the useful pieces of a collection of data. But the real brilliance of the relational model was revealed when more than one table was tied together with a common field. For example:

Names Table

Code	First	Surname	FirstPublished
1	Jim	Davis	1962
2	Mary	Seorle	1958
3	Bunny	Watson	1951

Work Table

Work	Poet_Code
Wakening Night	3
Thrones of Darkness	1
Once	2

Here, the Names table is related by the field Code to the Work table. Note how the author Jim Davis (the first row in the Names table) is entered only once and is referenced by the Poet_Code in the Work table. If, for example, Jim Davis really should be called *Jim Davey,* this entry needs to be changed in only one place, even if hundreds of his works have been added to the database.

Relational database applications may have hundreds or even thousands of such tables, and there is a trade-off between creating tables and breaking fields to such a low level that it stops being efficient. The process of separating out tables for storing data in a relation database is called *normalization,* and there are *forms* of normalization, such as 1st Normal Form, that refer to the extent to which data is parceled among the tables. At first glance, it might seem to make sense to totally eliminate any duplication, but this isn't always a good idea. For example, it doesn't make sense to break the FirstPublished column in the Poet table into its own table and then use some sort of code to maintain the relationship between tables because it is unlikely you would ever want to update entries as a whole.

Ironically, when Codd introduced the relational model, some thought that even the new mainframes would not be able to handle the overhead of keeping all the tables in sync. But the relational model had another feature that eventually made it hard to resist, and this was a standard for a query language.

Standard Query Language (SQL)

Relational databases allow you to perform the following data-manipulation functions:

- Retrieve data easily from a single table or groups of tables
- Create new tables
- Insert data into tables
- Update existing information in tables
- Add, delete, and modify columns of tables
- Delete rows from tables and tables as a whole

SQL provides a syntax for accomplishing these tasks that is remarkably consistent among different relational databases. SQL is known as a declarative query language. A *declarative language* allows users to express their wants, and then the system takes this expression and figures out how best to carry out the query. An SQL statement is an expression of a desired result, and the user or application that issues the statement does not need to know how the results are assembled. This allows an RDBMS to store the data however it chooses and allows RDBMS programmers to flex their mental muscles in coming up with more efficient ways of working with the data.

The most basic SQL statement is SELECT; following is an example:

```
SELECT * FROM POET
```

Most RDBMS do not require SQL statements to be in uppercase, and many developers use capitals for commands and tables, and lowercase for column/field specifications, but this is a matter of preference. The asterisk in the statement is a wildcard that indicates the system should return everything; that is, every field in each row. In this case, the results would be a list of the contents of the table.

Of course, you might decide you don't want to see everything, and SQL gives you the ability to specify which columns will be retrieved. For example:

```
SELECT surname FROM NAMES
```

You might then decide that you want the data in a particular order:

```
SELECT surname FROM WORKS ORDER BY SURNAME
```

Or that you also want to see the titles of works with names:

```
SELECT N.surname, W.title FROM NAMES AS N, WORKS AS W WHERE
N.code=W.poet_code ORDER BY SURNAME
```

SQL is a very flexible language and can go far beyond the examples given here. Although the basic syntax of SQL is consistent among different relational databases, RDBMSs often have their own peculiarities for *data types;* that is, the type of content that can be inserted into a field. The basic data types are as follows:

- Exact numerics, such as INTEGER for values like 42

- Approximate numerics for numbers that are either so large or so precise that they can't be represented by a computer; an approximation is used, such as REAL for values like 7.042E-23

- Character strings, most often VARCHAR, for values that vary in length, such as "Melville Dewey" and "West Virginia"

- Datetimes such as DATE for values like 2002-12-31

- Intervals for values that represent the difference between two datetime values, such as the number of days between two dates

The most variations in relational databases are in a special kind of data type called Binary Large Objects (BLOBs).[2] Relational databases typically have strict limits on field size; for instance, VARCHAR fields may be capped at 255 characters. Often BLOBS are the solution for storing content that can't be broken neatly into distinct fields. We see this in practice later.

One important SQL statement is the ALTER statement, which works with the MODIFY clause. Together, they allow incredible flexibility in storing data. For example, if you decide to store a Web address for each author, you can issue the following statement:

```
ALTER TABLE poet ADD url VARCHAR(25)
```

But wait! What if you discover that 25 characters isn't enough space for many of the URLs you must insert in the field? You can use the MODIFY clause to allocate a more generous default field size for storing data:

```
ALTER TABLE poet MODIFY url VARCHAR(255)
```

There are many esoteric SQL statements, and even though it is a very flexible model, certain types of content don't fit into it well. In the next section, we look at an open source RDBMS implementation that goes beyond SQL's limitations, making it an attractive option for almost any digital library collection.

MySQL

MySQL[3] has been called the "most popular database in the world,"[4] and with good reason: it is a relatively long-standing (in OSS terms) application with roots in the late eighties; it has been publicly available since 1996. In version 3.23, MySQL began to support full-text searching, a rare option in the OSS world of relational databases and a very welcome feature for supporting text-based collections. MySQL is available under the GPL license and runs on all major platforms

Consider a database that stores information about works by particular authors. You want the database to store the author's name, a URI that points to a Web resource about the author, a TIFF image of the original manuscript of the work, and the full text of the work. In MySQL syntax, the table definition looks like this:

```
CREATE TABLE works
(
   id int DEFAULT '0' NOT NULL AUTO_INCREMENT PRIMARY KEY,
   first_name varchar(30),
   middle_name varchar(30),
   last_name varchar(30),
   uri varchar(255),
   work_title varchar(255),
   work_blob longblob,
   work_text text,
   fulltext (first_name,middle_name,last_name,work_title,work_text)
);
```

Every database varies slightly in how tables are defined, and MySQL is no exception. The first field to define in the table, id, is the *primary key*; that is, it uniquely identifies every row that is added to the table. Because authors' names are different sizes, you estimate a large enough number of characters for the maximum entry the database accepts. For both the title of the work and the URI, you use the largest amount that MySQL allows for a VARCHAR field.

When you reach the work_blob field, you really start delving into database-specific aspects of MySQL. You define this field as a *longblob*, which can hold a binary file up to 4 gigabytes in size. This is the largest setting allowed in MySQL and highlights the importance of scoping out the content that will be added to a database. If you plan to store TIFF images for large manuscripts or a really massive amount of content such as full-motion video, you must consider options such as breaking the file into multiple fields or storing a URI that points to the object. There are multimedia functions in some relational databases that can take advantage of binary data, but usually, placing a large object in a table simplifies finding and managing it.

Like blobs, the text data type in MySQL can be defined in multiple ways. The text type is, in fact, a form of blob, and the only difference is that MySQL treats it as a case-insensitive field so that values like "cat" and "CAT" are considered identical when performing searches.

Finally, tell MySQL you want a full-text index on all of the fields that will store character data with the FULLTEXT command. The command to add content to the table looks like this:

```
INSERT INTO works VALUES(0,'Jack','Griffith','London',
'http://www.jacklondon.net',
'Brown Wolf',
LOAD_FILE("/tmp/brown_wolf.tiff") ,
'BROWN WOLF
She had delayed, because of the dew-wet grass, in order to put on her
overshoes, and when she emerged from the house found her waiting husband
absorbed in the wonder of a bursting almond-bud. She sent a questing
glance across the tall grass and in and out among the orchard trees…');
```

Since you told MySQL to autoincrement the id field, you can pass it a value of 0 and it will take care of updating the field to the appropriate value. The trickiest part of this command is LOAD_FILE. MySQL must be given the full path to the file or it will assume that you really want nothing in the field. The path in the example is for a UNIX system; if you are using a Windows operating system, the path must be specified like this:

```
LOAD_FILE("\\tmp\\brown_wolf.tiff")
```

Note the double slash (\\). MySQL uses a slash to *escape* a character that has special meaning to it. By using the slash, you are telling MySQL to treat the character following the slash as part of the field's value. This is particularly important when dealing with text. For example, consider the following sentence:

```
'Mine is no futility of genius that can't sell gems to the magazines.'
```

An apostrophe is a special character in MySQL. When MySQL arrives at the word *can't*, it gets confused about whether the apostrophe in the word indicates that the field ends there. To avoid an error message, you must use the slash escape character to tell MySQL to keep going and adding the rest of the characters to the field:

```
'Mine is no futility of genius that can\'t sell gems to the magazines.'
```

Of course, the advantages of using MySQL don't really show until it is time to pull information out of the database. Use the SELECT statement for this:

```
SELECT work_title FROM works WHERE MATCH(first_name,middle_name,last_name,
work_title,work_text) AGAINST ('overshoes');
```

Presuming the table contains only one story with a reference to overshoes, the results are as follows:

```
+--------------+
| work_title  |
+--------------+
| Brown Wolf  |
+--------------+
```

The full-text options tend to be verbose, and many times using the field names directly accomplishes a task. For example, you might use the following query to pull out all the materials by Jack London:

```
SELECT work_title FROM works WHERE first_name='Jack' AND
last_name='London'
```

Note that the first name "Jack" and the last name "London" are in mixed case; that is, they match the format in which they were entered into the database. MySQL usually gives the same results for the following query:

```
SELECT work_title FROM works WHERE first_name='JACK' AND
last_name='LONDON'
```

However, not all relational databases will treat the preceding two queries as equivalent. If you suspect that you will use VARCHAR fields for the bulk of your information requests, consider adding an entry that applies a set of rules for handling characters, a process sometimes called *normalization,* though, in this case, the goal is provide a reasonable expectation of what entries might be retrieved with rather than relating tables to each other.

To see how this normalization might be implemented, consider a table with the following definition:

```
CREATE TABLE works
(
   id                 int DEFAULT '0' NOT NULL AUTO_INCREMENT PRIMARY KEY,
   last_name          varchar(30),
   normal_last_name   varchar(30),
   ...
```

Now consider names like *Jack O'Brien* or authors with special characters in their names, such as *Nikolai Vorobév*. The table entries might look like the following:

id	last_name	normal_last_name
1	O'Brien	O BRIEN
2	Vorobév	VOROBEV
...		

A search interface built on top of the database is able to take queries entered as "O'Brien" and "O Brien" and retrieve data from the database using "O BRIEN." Normalizing terms is an incredibly useful method for matching queries against the content of a database.

Other OSS Relational Databases

Given the popularity of MySQL, you might wonder why you would even consider using a different RDBMS. Despite MySQL's many strengths and almost unbeatable performance, it is not always an appropriate solution. Table 5.1 lists a few other options to consider (for detailed information, refer to the Further Resources section).

There are companies that sell commercial support for MySQL and PostgreSQL, and SAP DB and Interbase have support options from their original creators. Product support is probably the key distinction between these databases: a complex installation with many users updating records might cause you to look closely at the support contract. In general, digital library applications tend to be used much less for additions to the database than for retrieving content, and much of the higher-end referential integrity features are not needed for the bulk of the database's use.

Putting It All Together

Relational databases are based on a powerful data model, and SQL provides a useful means of extracting and maintaining digital content. MySQL is an excellent open source RDBMS for digital library projects, and there other several other strong relational databases to choose from. An RDBMS provides a mechanism for storing and retrieving objects in a digital collection using long-standing and well-understood approaches to working with data.

Table 5.1. Popular OSS Relational Databases

Database	Platform	Notes	License
HSQL	Java-based, every major platform	A very small and compact database, HSQL is a good choice for a small collection (less than 500 entries), particularly if you want to easily distribute the database to several users.	Custom GPL-style license
PostgreSQL	All major platforms, including Mac OS X	More complex than MySQL, particularly for BLOBs, PostgreSQL is a good choice for a complex table structure and/or if you suspect you will have many concurrent users updating tables.	BSD
SAP DB	Windows, Linux, some other variants of UNIX	Since version 7.2, SAP DB has been transformed from a commercial database to an OSS system. It is a well-documented and mature database. Option for commercial support directly from original company.	GNU Lesser General Public License
Interbase/ Firebird	Windows, Solaris, Linux	Like SAP DB, Interbase has commercial roots and is a solid database. Option for commercial support directly from original company. Firebird seems to have a stronger OSS community connection.	Mozilla
Berkley DB	Windows and UNIX; source compilation required	Berkeley DB is a powerful database but geared toward developers. XML support was added recently. Perl and other scripting environments can be used, but Berkley DB does not support SQL directly.	Custom GPL-style

6 Object and XML Databases

As we discussed in the last chapter, some types of content may not benefit from the relational model. Many database experts make the distinction between *data-centric* and *document-centric* information; data-centric content more often is designed for machine consumption, and documents usually are designed for humans to read.[1] MySQL blurs the distinction somewhat by adding support for full-text documents, but even with MySQL, the content usually requires some amount of manipulation to make it suitable to insert into a table.

Object and XML databases typically are more ready "out of the box" to accept content without requiring the data to be changed internally; that is, the content usually goes into the database as a whole and comes out as a whole. OAI repositories and DL-specific systems may go even further in this direction, with the bulk of setup and customization requiring very little manipulation of the underlying data model. Similarly, Object/Relational databases blur all distinctions by being document-friendly, while also supporting relational tables.

Generally, an object or XML database is one in which the system is a container for a *logical* model of the content—as opposed to the data in the object—and works with the document based on that model; for example, using XPath instead of SQL to pull together XML content. Although SQL is very powerful, it really works best with content that can be broken into small units without requiring an inordinate number of columns and that typically is modified field by field. An XML document or TIFF image usually is manipulated as a stand-alone object; in fact, validation cannot easily occur for an XML document unless you have all of its fields and most graphic programs can't easily deal with anything but a complete image. Still, whether an RDBMS is on the back end or a line of mice handing paper to each other, as long as the object appears when requested, it fills the role of an object container.

Also, repositories and XML/object databases often are used to add a layer of management to the workflow of an object rather than directly to the object itself; for example, tracking multiple versions of an XML file or image, or passing the object through a series of editors before making it widely available. Some object databases have special functions to deal with particular kinds of content; for example, compressing image data. Finally, object/XML and prepackaged databases typically are much easier to install and implement quickly. Defining relations in an RDBMS usually takes time and experimentation to decide on judicious parceling of data across tables. The systems described in this chapter typically can save you this effort.

Zope

Zope[2] is considered one of the world's first *application servers*,[3] a somewhat confusing class of systems that designates an application to act as a Web server while providing special tools for bringing content to the Web. At its heart is a powerful object database that presents the Web server as a sort of directory-based desktop. For example, Figure 6.1 resembles the display when you log in to Zope.

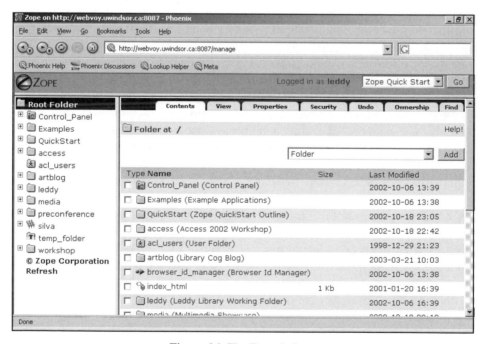

Figure 6.1. The Zope desktop.

If you use a directory tool such as File Manager or Windows Explorer, this view will seem familiar. Zope leverages the concept of folders for organizing content and adding applications. This is a huge benefit to most Zope users since it taps into a well-understood means of managing content.

Zope is quite well documented and makes it very easy to create a Web-based application. It is made available under a custom GPL-style license and is usually a breeze to install on most platforms. Zope has great support for defining user permissions so that multiple users can work on a project, and it has numerous prebuilt tools for everything from building blogs (weblogs that are updated frequently) to portals. The information in the Further Resources section will get you started using Zope for developing Web applications. What we concentrate on in this chapter is using Zope for XML content, an area in which the available documentation is still evolving and where Zope is of special interest for digital libraries.

Using XML in Zope

Zope was one of the first application servers to use XML, and Python, the scripting environment in which Zope is built, is a preferred programming language for many XML developers. Despite this, at the time of this writing, XML support in Zope requires two building blocks not prepackaged with the Zope distribution. These are PyXML,[4] a Python-based XML toolkit, and 4Suite,[5] a comprehensive XML/RDF suite. Be aware that the current version of Zope (2.5.1) must run on Python 2.1, even though the latest release of Python is 2.2.

Adding PyXML and 4Suite to your environment is usually straightforward in Linux and most forms of UNIX. In Windows environments, it is easier to use a full Python distribution, which is available from the main Python Web site.[6] If you are using the Windows operating system, install the Python 2.1 distribution and then navigate to the directory where you installed Zope. There, you can edit the Start.bat file to use the full Python distribution just installed. This typically involves changing the following line:

```
"C:\Program Files\zope\bin\python.exe" "C:\Program Files\
zope\z2.py" -D %1 %2 …
```

to:

```
"C:\python21\python.exe" "C:\Program Files\zope\z2.py"
-D %1 %2 …
```

Try running Zope with these changes to make sure it functions. Then you can install PyXML and 4Suite directly.

With PyXML and 4Suite in place, you can retrieve the two Zope applications that integrate XML into Zope. In Zope parlance, applications to be used with Zope are called *Products;* Zope has many XML Products in addition to what is described here. Despite the preparation needed to get the environment ready for them, the Products we will use, ParsedXML[7] and XSL Transform,[8] are considered the most fully developed options for XML in Zope. They follow the standard Zope install method of being unzipped/untarred to the Products directory.

Windows users must edit the XMLTransform.py file in the directory in which XSL Transform was unzipped and verify that the correct version of the 4Suite tool is used. Make sure the uncommented line, that is, the one without the number sign (#), is available as shown:

```
# Which transformer do you want?
# Leave your choice uncommented, with the rest commented out
# Future TBD: make this a property file setting so
# no Python source code has to be changed.
#
#from LibXsltProcessor import LibXsltProcessor as XSLTProcessor
from FourSuite12Processor import FourSuite12Processor as XSLTProcessor
```

With this in place, you have the option to add ParsedXML and XMLTransform content to a Zope folder. The documentation for these tools will get you started. At this point, XSL Transform cannot yet work directly with ParsedXML. An easy way to work around this is to reference the ParsedXML content directly from a Document Template Markup Language (DTML) document, which is a type of document specific to Zope, and which designates an object that can contain HTML while supporting special tags for additional Zope functionality.

For example, if your XML content were contained in a ParsedXML object called eric, you would create a DTML document called, for example, Deric.xml with the following contents:

```
<dtml-var expr="eric.index_html()">
```

This tells Zope to use the default view of the eric object. By using Deric.xml when specifying what content the stylesheet(s) should work with, you can take advantage of XSL Transform's sophisticated caching mechanisms and other features (see Figure 6.2). A future release of ParsedXML should support the method required by XML Transform, so hopefully the DTML detour is a temporary workaround. Zope also has a product called XMLKit[9] that is a more lightweight toolkit than ParsedXML, but it can't be used with Zope's search engine.

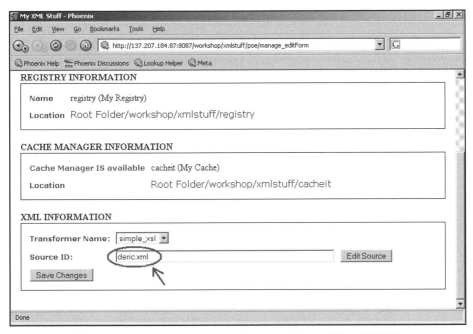

Figure 6.2. Using XML Transform to associate a stylesheet with an XML document.

Using Zope for XML Searching

Searching Zope objects involves using a Product called Zcatalog.[10] Zope also includes tools for automatically building a search interface and navigating through large results. To support searching XML documents, you must create a Zcatalog for ParsedXML content. To do this, add a Zcatalog to the folder where your documents are stored. It is important to go into the Indexes tab and define a TextIndex with the name *nodeValue* as shown in Figure 6.3.

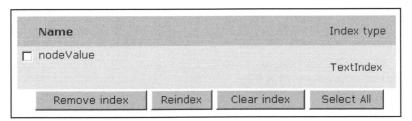

Figure 6.3. Using the Indexer tab in Zcatalog.

Without nodeValue, Zope will gladly churn through the document but won't add the actual content to the catalogue without this index. Select the Metadata tab and at least include the bobobase_modification_time and id. These are values that refer to the time the entry is updated and how to retrieve from the underlying object database. Some of the other values won't match anything in

ParsedXML, and you may find it useful to add nodeValue here as well. This comes in handy if you want to see what is coming back easily using the automatically generated search forms. The Metadata list should have at least the entries shown in Figure 6.4.

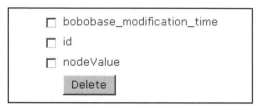

Figure 6.4. Inside the Metadata tab in Zcatalog.

There are two script files, called catalogIt and walkTree, available on the book's Web site as zexp files that walk through XML content. The zexp format is Zope's export file mechanism and can be imported directly to the Zcatalog folder. You must modify catalogIt to reflect which document you are working on as shown in the following code in bold:

```
start = container.eric.documentElement
theLastNode= container.walkTree(start,"","/dl/workingfolder/eric")
```

Select the Test tab and look at the Catalog tab (see Figure 6.5). You will see that the document has been indexed by reference to its Document Object Model (DOM) object.

ZCatalog at /workshop/testing/mycat	Help!
mycat contains 30 record(s).	
[Next 10 entries]	
Object Identifier	**Type**
☐ /workshop/testing/eric/0/1/0	ZCatalog
☐ /workshop/testing/eric/0/3/0	ZCatalog
☐ /workshop/testing/eric/0/4	ZCatalog
☐ /workshop/testing/eric/0/5/0/0	ZCatalog

Figure 6.5. DOM entries in Zcatalog.

This demonstrates one of the unique aspects of ParsedXML: every section of a document can be referenced independently and accessed from the database, instead of requiring that the entire document be loaded before drilling down to a particular section. This is useful if you want to display a subset of a large document in your search results or use URLs that reference each section of the document. Once you have built a Zcatalog, there are good examples in the general Zope documentation and in information in the Further Resources section that explain how to make the content available to your users.

Zope is a very powerful system, and currently there are initiatives under way to make using XML in Zope more straightforward.[11] But even with these extra steps, it can be well worth the effort to use Zope for XML content because it is so effective at managing content and workflows.

Xindice

It would be hard to imagine a more "XML-centric" database system than Xindice.[12] It uses XPath as a query language and works with any well-formed XML document. Xindice comes from the Apache Foundation and is bundled with several of Apache's XML projects, including Cocoon. Like Cocoon, Xindice uses the Apache license and requires Java as well as some planning for the layout of your collection. In Xindice, documents are stored in *collections*, and the collections are defined by a layout that resembles a file directory. For example, you might have a collection on travel logs as part of a general collection.To Xindice, this looks like the following:

```
/general-collection/travel-logs
```

Working with Xindice generally means working from the command line. For example, you can add the document pacific_coast_1883.xml to the collection with the following command:

```
xindice add_document  c /general collection/
travel-logs -f pacific_coast_1883.xml
```

Chances are, you will want to add many documents to a collection at once and you will have a particular directory structure in place for managing the XML content. If you wanted to add all the files in a directory called /work/xmlfiles, you could do this with the following command:

```
xindice add_multiple_documents -c /general-collection/ travel-logs -f
/work/xmlfiles
```

Or, you might want to add only files with the extension .xml:

```
xindice add_multiple_documents -c /general-collection/ travel-logs -f
/work/xmlfiles -e xml
```

Xindice can assign *keys* for your documents, or you can assign your own. If you are constantly updating files, or if you already assign some sort of ID to the file, you can tell Xindice to use that as a key with the -n parameter:

```
xindice add_document -c /general-collection/
travel-logs -f pacific_coast_1883.xml -n travel001
```

The key is handy if you want to update or delete individual documents. You also may choose to delete collections and rebuild them periodically. Since Xindice stores a copy of the content, this can work well, but if you habitually remove files after you work on them, be sure to remember that Xindice can't rebuild what is no longer there.

Perhaps the biggest advantage of Xindice is its support of XPath. XPath can be a very powerful tool for information retrieval. For example, if you want to find all the documents that are inventories, use the following command:

```
xindice xpath -c /general-collection/travel-logs -q
"/eadheader/archdesc[@type='inventory']"
```

Of course, your users probably will not type queries from the command line, and you will be working with either a scripting language (see Chapter 8) or using an environment like Cocoon that helps set up an interactive query system. Xindice also has a very solid Java-based API if you have access to a Java programmer.

Other OSS Object/XML Databases

Databases and XML modeling tools such as Castor[13] and Hibernate[14] are not included in Table 6.1 because they require a deep level of programming. The listed systems can either be easily scripted or have fairly minimal requirements to implement; see the Further Resources section for more information.

Putting It All Together

Object/XML databases are well suited for digital collections in which the content is best handled as a series of stand-alone objects. Zope is a strong object-based database system for storing and managing digital content and can be leveraged to work with XML. Xindice is a flexible XML database system that can offer XPath as a searching layer. There are not many options in the open source world for object/XML database solutions, but with the popularity of XML, this is likely to be a growing area of OSS development.

Table 6.1. Object/XML Systems and Toolkits

Database	Platform	Notes	Type	License
eXist	Java-base, all major platforms	eXist features tight integration with Cocoon; it is very similar to Xindice.	XML	GPL
4Suite	Windows, Linux, other UNIX systems (with tweaking)	4Suite offers database support as part of a suite of tools for XML and RDF processing. A must have for Python programmers.	XML/RDF	Custom Apache-style license
Ozone	Java-based	Ozone is still geared toward Java programmers at the time of this writing, but work is ongoing to expose objects through SQL. It is a sophisticated system in an area where there is not yet a lot of OSS options.	Object	GPL

7 | Built to Order: DL-Specific Systems

Not surprisingly, digital library architects seem to be naturally committed to information dissemination, and systems that have been built specifically for digital library projects tend to be made publicly available so that others can take advantage of the work that has been carried out in the project. This chapter gives a brief introduction to some options, but you are encouraged to consult the extensive documentation available for each application if it sounds like a match for a particular collection or project.

Please note that there are systems that might be considered digital libraries that harvest or focus on remote Web-based resources, and these have not been described here. Such applications are obviously of great value, but this starts to step over into general Web application space, where describing potential systems would take several volumes. Content Management Systems (CMS)[1] and library-specific virtual library tools such as iVia[2] are well worth pursuing in these areas.

The systems selected here share the requirement that they support local collections and content. The trade-off between one of these systems and a more generic database really comes down to three areas:

1. Support. General open source database systems may often have a larger community of users and offer more assurance than software that is maintained and developed for a narrower purpose.

2. Missing features. Adding the one or two missing features to an application that has already been tailored to a specific purpose may not be as easy as implementing one made available with the expectation that it will be customized.

3. Management. Many digital library systems are geared toward self-contained content; that is, content that is *ready for dissemination at the time of entry*. In a more generic system such as Zope, for example, it is possible to assign an *editing* cycle, so that the content goes through a series of authors/editors before it is made available, and it can be subject to active change while residing in the system.

The nature of the content and the digital library project likely will be the deciding factors in your approach. Generally, if you are under a tight deadline, these systems, particularly the ones that have been in use for some time, are probably what you are looking for.

dlbox

The dlbox, or "Digital Libraries–in-a-Box," project is distributed by the Digital Library Research Laboratory at Virginia Tech.[3] It utilizes extensions to the OAI Protocol for Metadata Harvesting (XOAI-PMH) to support component-to-component integration. We examine components in Chapter 9, but the concept is similar to using a child's collection of building blocks. Small, well-defined blocks allow very intricate and widely varying structures, and dlbox allows tremendous flexibility in designing a digital library. The components available as part of dlbox are listed in Table 7.1.

Table 7.1. The Components of a dlbox

Component	Description
IRDB Search Engine	A search engine based on an OAI-accessible data archive, capable of submitting queries and retrieving results.
DBBrowse Browse Engine	A browsing system based on the use of categories in the metadata.
OAIB	The heart of dlbox, this is the server and requires an SQL-capable server, such as MySQL, and a servlet container, such as Tomcat.
DBUnion Archive Merger Component	Merges OAI and XOAI-PMH archives together for local storage and processing.
XML File	As seen in Chapter 3, this adds OAI support to a set of XML files.
Submit Archive Component	XOAI-PHM requires the ability to "put" a record in an archive, something that is not supported in the current OAI protocol. This component supplies this functionality.
Threaded Annotation Engine	A custom annotation engine, this allows external annotations to be applied to any resource.
What's New Engine	Supports a listing of a new or random set of records through OAI.
MDEdit XML Schema-based Metadata Editor	Web-form-based metadata editor.
Grunk	The Grammar Understanding Kernel is an application from NCSA to extract metadata from text file documents without existing metadata.

The components can be downloaded individually and largely are built with Perl and Java tools. If you have already built a structure for a digital collection in a relational database, these components can be used to apply additional functionality to your existing setup. Dr. Edward Fox, one of the researchers behind this project, is a leading figure in the digital library world and is closely involved with many high-profile DL projects, including the National Science Digital Library (NSDL).[4] The Web site for this project includes a full tutorial that walks a user through creating a digital library from scratch.

DL Generator

The DL Generator system is also a project from Virginia Tech under the direction of Edward Fox. The generator is based on 5S Language (5SL), an XML realization of a conceptual model of digital libraries known as 5S,[5] which represents streams, structure, spaces, scenarios, and societies (see Table 7.2).

Table 7.2. The Models That Make Up 5S

5S	Description
Stream model	Properties of the digital contents supported by the digital library, such as text and video. 5SL uses standard MIME types to express the *stream;* for example, the image/GIF.
Structural model	Specifies the structures used in the 5S model, such as the internal structure of a digital object, as well as metadata standards and organizational tools.
Spatial model	Logical and presentational views of the content.
Scenarios model	Describes the behavior of DL services, such as an action that takes place to provide a service; for example, generate an image based on a user request.
Societies model	Defines the roles of participants in digital library activities, such as managers (who run the service) and actors (who use the service).

The DL Generator leverages MARIAN,[6] a digital library system developed at Virginia Tech's Digital Library Research Laboratory, to provide information retrieval functionality on the basis of protocols such as Z39.50 and its own facilities for dealing with content types such as XML and general text. An intriguing premise of the DL Generator is that a designer will formalize a conceptual description using 5S, and this description will allow the generator to produce the complete application using MARIAN and other component sources.

At the time of this writing, the DL Generator had not yet been made available for public release, but it could greatly change the nature of how digital library applications are constructed. The 5S model also represents a rich model for describing existing digital libraries and has possibilities for resource discovery and service sharing between digital collections.

Fedora

The Flexible Extensible Digital Object and Repository Architecture (Fedora) originates with Cornell's Digital Library Research Group, and the current system is maintained in partnership with the University of Virginia, using funding from the Andrew M. Mellon Foundation.[7] Fedora was released as an open source project in mid-2003 and represents a sophisticated and mature architecture for storing digital objects. Fedora has adopted METS to manage objects as XML entities and exposes digital objects through a persistent ID (PID) so that they can be referenced in URIs. Object-related services are also URI-addressable; for example, a URL to get a thumbnail of an image.

Fedora uses the concept of *data streams* to represent the different formats of the content of an object, *disseminators* for manifesting a view of the content, and *behaviors* to define the methods for presenting or transforming the content (see Figure 7.1). Content and services can be accessed with both GET/POST requests and using SOAP.

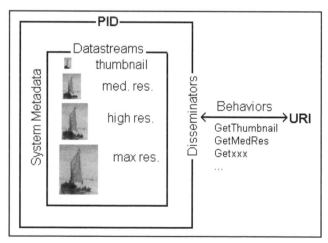

Figure 7.1. Fedora exposes content through URIs. Different behaviors are defined to allow a Web client to request the available views of the content.

Cornell and the University of Virginia represent two of the largest and most active digital library groups, and Fedora has been eagerly anticipated. The architecture behind the system is well documented and the Fedora project already has made an invaluable contribution to the digital library field by successfully introducing the notion of a disseminator into the METS schema. This positions METS to work well with Web-based technologies, for which it is often essential that behaviors and services be associated with objects.

Greenstone

Greenstone is one of the most popular and well-known digital library systems, and with good reason: it is a comprehensive and well-thought-out application with a strong track record in delivering content. Greenstone supports multiple *collections,* each of which can have their own about page and customized indexing appropriate to the content of the collection. It uses its own markup language (Greenstone Markup Language, or GML), which can include any metadata associated with the document. Files are stored in a separate directory for each collection, and the system has a special indexing setup to automatically update changes to files and then copy over the index. Like many specialized file-indexing systems, Greenstone has very impressive performance and great keyword support; but unlike many indexing systems, it also includes strong facilities for browsing. Greenstone uses the Unicode[8] character set and shines for multilanguage collections (see Figure 7.2).

Figure 7.2. Greenstone in action.

In addition to powering the New Zealand Digital Library,[9] Greenstone is used for collections all over the world.[10] It has been deployed on most major platforms and has facilities for end-user collection building[11] so that digital libraries can be constructed in a distributed fashion. Greenstone is available under a GPL license.

SiteSearch

In June 2001, OCLC announced that SiteSearch,[12] a suite of information management and retrieval tools, would no longer be available as a commercial product. With the release of version 4.0.2a in May 2002, SiteSearch was made available under the OCLC Open Source license and is one of the few examples in the library world of a commercial product becoming open source. SiteSearch has a strong Z39.50 layer and can provide one interface to local and remote collections (see Figure 7.3). Many converters and other tools are available for transferring content into SiteSearch, and it can directly index MARC, XML, and SGML formats.

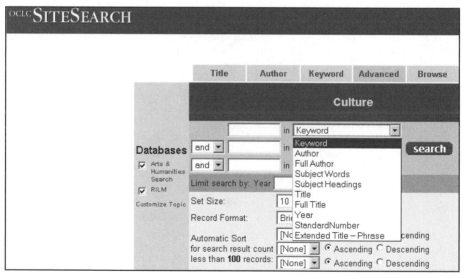

Figure 7.3. SiteSearch in action.
Note the variety of search options and the ability to search across databases.

SiteSearch is very quick to get running "out of the box" with its default templates, yet it allows for extensive customization. Although some Perl scripts are used for some content formatting and other tasks, SiteSearch is built largely with Java. The documentation identifies several UNIX and Windows platforms for deploying SiteSearch, and it uses OCLC's own license.

Putting It All Together

dlbox, and possibly the DL Generator at some point, is a good option to consider if you are using an existing system or plan to use a relational database for your digital collection. The component approach championed by Virginia Tech lends itself to utilization for systems that are not necessarily built by the same tools. The 5S model is a much-needed formal model for digital libraries. Regardless of whether the DL Generator becomes popular for building collections when it becomes available, it could still be an invaluable planning tool.

For getting a project going quickly, Greenstone and SiteSearch have both proved capable of handling diverse content, and there are numerous active deployments of these systems to comfort those who want tried-and-true solutions. Fedora represents an interesting combination of a system that currently works with large deployed collections while having the hooks through URIs for use with components. The open source release of Fedora has been eagerly awaited, and various demonstration implementations may be available by the time you read this.

8

Scripting Languages and Regular Expressions

Almost all computer applications are built using programming languages. Even a firmware system contains a program that is usually built with a specific type of language. The language offers a formal method for directing the computer to perform certain tasks through a series of statements. Depending on the vintage of the programming language and the clarity of the programmer, these statements may be somewhat meaningful to the casual reader or be completely indecipherable.

Figure 8.1 shows some snippets of code from two longstanding programming languages. The first is written in assembly language and refers directly to a computer's instruction set and storage areas (registers) used within a computer's central processing unit (CPU) to carry out tasks. Assembly language programs are written very close to computer hardware, and very few programmers today work at this level when designing applications. The second example is written in a language called C, one of the first and most popular programming languages to combine the power of assembly language with a more human-friendly syntax. C, and its more modern successor, C++, power the bulk of computer applications on the planet.

It would not be unreasonable to expect the assembly language program to be more difficult to follow than the C program, and this is generally the case, but the traditional programming approaches to getting a computer to do useful work can be intimidating with either of these tools.[1]

Listing 1	Listing 2

``
JMP   01BA   ;Have storage
CS: ;New INT 8
CMP   WO [010A],4000 ;Check for
FLAG
JZ   0127   ;Set second
escape key
CS:
CMP   WO [010A],+00   ;If 0,
initialize counter
JZ   012C
CS:
DEC   WO [010A]   ;Decrement
JNZ   0133
``
	``
	if (strlen(value) > 1) {
	    while (*whereisimage[i] != '\0')
	{
	        if (strstr(whereisimage[i],
	        value))
	        {
	            fprintf(fp,"available");
	        } else {
	            fprintf(fp,"not
	available") ;
	        }
	        i++;
	    }
	}
	``

Figure 8.1. Code from familiar programming languages.

The Role of Scripting Languages

As the preceding examples imply, delivering computer applications can require a deep understanding of the underlying hardware and operating system. Today, digital library projects can make good use of open source tools that can deliver amazing computing power at a fraction of the complexity associated with traditional programming languages. These tools are a class of applications known as *scripting languages*. The definition of what constitutes a scripting language is not completely clear. An oft-used criterion is that an application designed with a programming language is usually *compiled* into a format that is linked to the tools needed by the operating system to work directly with the machine instructions needed by the hardware. The result is that a compiled program can run directly without requiring a special environment beyond the operating system.

With a scripting language, on the other hand, the language is usually *interpreted* as it executes and the scripting environment provides the linking for the operating system. This is slower than a compiled application because the *interpreter* must examine each statement in the program every time it is executed and then invoke the desired action by the operating system, whereas the compiled code just performs the action directly. Scripting solutions are typically much less efficient than compiled programs, but usually save developers tremendous time in putting together applications. Also, the distinctions between scripting and other kinds of applications are not always absolute; tools to compile scripting languages are now available, and some programming environments, such as Java, use an interpreter for what comes out of the compiler rather than for the statements that are used in the program.

For our purposes, a scripting language usually has the following characteristics:

- It is easier to use than other types of programming languages.[2]
- It is well suited to small projects and tying together systems that can do the "heavy lifting" for an application.
- It probably is not the tool of choice for low-level applications such as device drivers and compute-intensive programs like mathematical number crunching.
- It typically is excellent for Web applications (in which the latency of the network is far more of an issue than the speed of the application).
- It typically is excellent at handling text because scripting languages have often been developed specifically with text-based tasks in mind.

It is the last two points that make scripting languages of special interest for those working with digital libraries. Digital libraries usually are wired firmly into the Web and often need to process great quantities of text for digital collections; for example, converting a mass of individual text files created with optical character recognition (OCR) into a more malleable format for human editing. Some scripting languages are also suited for diverse non-Web or -text functions, such as building graphical interfaces in TCL/TK[3] and adding browser-based functionality with JavaScript,[4] but we look at three of the leading contenders for "best OSS DL scripting language." By strange coincidence, they all begin with the letter "*p*."

Perl

The Practical Extraction and Report Language or the Pathologically Eclectic Rubbish Lister (Perl)[5] is a scripting language created by Larry Wall in 1987. Perl was originally designed to be a quick and easy tool to extract information from text files and generate reports. One of Larry Wall's stated design goals was to make easy tasks easy and difficult tasks possible. Some would argue that Perl really revolutionized the notion of a modern scripting language, and it remains one of the most popular tools for gluing together applications that were not originally designed to work together.

Perl is available under the Artistic License and GPL; it is also available for most operating systems. One of its strengths is the huge collection of freely usable perl add-ons, or *modules,* that are available for it, including modules that allow database systems to be manipulated easily in a script. These often are downloaded from a network of sites called CPAN.[6] Most of the modules on CPAN are also available under the Artistic License, the GPL, or both.

What it looks like:

```
# A sample Perl program

$_ = "Welcome to Our Digital Collections!";
print;
```

And its output:

```
Welcome to Our Digital Collections!
```

PHP

The PHP: Hypertext Preprocessor (known simply as PHP)[7] is primarily used for server-side Web scripts. A server-side Web application is one that is executed on the Web server and the results of the application are then delivered to the browser. Commercial alternatives to server-side Web development using scripts are available, such as Microsoft's Active Server Pages (ASP)[8] system, but PHP is widely considered the most popular tool for Web scripting.[9] PHP began in 1994 when a Web developer named Rasmus Lerdof was formalizing the collection of Perl scripts he created for use on his home page; in fact, the first meaning for PHP was "Personal Home Page" tools. PHP is made available under a custom Apache-style license and is available for all major platforms.

Given the Web-centric nature of its origins, it is not surprising that PHP shines for easy integration into HTML. For example, an HTML page could contain a PHP program like the following:

```
<HTML>
<?php
    echo "<title>Welcome to Our Digital Collections!</title>";
?>
</HTML>
```

PHP has many built-in functions for Web applications. For example, changing characters in a URL so that their hexadecimal values can be passed over the Web is a common task when using complex URLs. Examples are functions for encoding and decoding special characters in URLs; for example, http://www.hollywood.org/tributes/John&Wayne is decoded to become http://www.hollywood.org/tributes/John&Wayne for viewing.

Like Perl, PHP easily can interact with a very large number of database systems. It is particularly well suited for working with MySQL, and the PHP/MySQL combination is a popular building block for many database driven Web sites.

Python

Python[10] was created by a developer named Guido van Rossum in 1991, and despite the multitude of serpent graphics evidenced on Python publications and Web sites, Python is named after the television series *Monty Python's Flying Circus*. Python most often is defined by how it differs from Perl; in fact, it often has been described as a more "spare" or "object" approach to Perl's somewhat elaborate syntax.

Python is more stringent about data types, such as integers, so that there is less chance of making mistakes like "1 + O" as opposed "1 + 0" (hint: one expression uses the letter "*o*" instead of the number "0"; almost every developer loses several hours hunting down a bug like this at some point in his or her natural life). Python also insists on a syntax that forces code to be more cleanly laid out than is required in other environments.

What it looks like:

```
def welcome():
    print "Welcome to Our Digital Collections!"
```

With Python, tabs must be used in statements, and it lends itself to defining functions or objects that can be reused for putting together applications, in this example, an admittedly not very useful function called *welcome*. Python almost forces you to think of parceling up tasks into reusable pieces, which can save you enormous effort as you move through a large project.

Scripting Digital Libraries

Most popular scripting languages are very well documented, and a plethora of useful tutorials on getting started with a particular scripting language exists, including several described in the Further Resources section. It would be hard not to gain some benefit in learning any of the languages described here, and the decision on which one to use may be more dependent on local experience and resources. For example, if you have access to a Perl wizard in your organization, this might be a huge incentive to work in Perl because you can probably tap into in-house expertise.

So many common computer tasks have been tackled with scripts that you may find it will be more a question of slightly modifying code that already exists rather than writing everything from scratch. Digital collections involve so many different kinds of tasks that it is hard to imagine where learning a scripting language would never be of use. Even with the most packaged digital library system available, you may need to put together an online survey on its current layout or may want to add a new layer of services to the Web site for the collection. Scripting languages empower you to stretch the boundaries of what you can offer in your digital library project.

Regular Expressions

Perl, PHP, Python, and many other scripting languages share one characteristic that supercharge them for dealing with text, and that is built-in support for regular expressions. *Regular expressions* (sometimes abbreviated to *regex* or *regexp*) refer to rules that work with sets of characters, known as *strings*. Regular expressions derive their name from the mathematical theory behind them.

The beginnings of regular expressions go back to a mathematician named Stephen Kleene, who described models of the nervous system using a mathematical notation called regular sets. Ken Thompson, one of the inventors of the UNIX operating system, decided to build this notation into a number of UNIX tools, in particular, a command-line tool called grep, which became the primary introduction to regular expressions for many programmers.[11]

To understand why regular expressions are so useful, it is worth looking at common problems that occur with large collections of textual material. For example, suppose you want to identify every section of text that mentions specific times, like 10:23 and 11:30, in order to put together a diary of events from the papers of an organization. The regular expression for this might look like the following:

```
[0-9]?[0-9]:[0-9][0-9]
```

The brackets "([])" in regular expressions denote a *character group* or *character class*, in this case, a range of characters so that the numbers 0 through 9 are considered valid matches. The "question mark (?)" character means that zero or one more characters can follow it if they meet the criterion that comes next, in this case, the second "[]" character class for limiting valid characters to falling between "0" and "9". Regular expressions allow ranges to be specified with the "hyphen (-)" character; for example, "[a-zA-Z]" will match any alphabetic character. Table 8.1 gives some of the most common syntaxes used in regular expressions.

If you wanted to identify certain strings in your text and you use a UNIX environment, you probably wouldn't need to go beyond the grep command for many tasks, but the combination of a scripting language and regular expressions is what gives you the tools for transforming a large mass of text into usable content. This is particularly important when dealing with OCR and other technologies that produce plain text, since it is likely the results will need some massaging before they are ready for inclusion in a digital collection.

Table 8.1. Common Syntaxes

.	A period matches any single character. For example: *T.m* will match both *Tim* and *Tom*.
( )	Parentheses group one or more regular expressions together as a single expression. For example, *(b.gfoo.)* will match *bigfoot* but not *brigfood*.
*	An asterisk matches zero or more occurrences of the expression that precedes it. For example, *a*'* matches the strings *a*, *aaa*, and ""*(empty string)*.
+	A plus sign matches one or more occurrences of the expression that precedes it. For example, *a+* matches the strings *a* and *aaaaaa*, but not "" (the empty string), since at least one occurrence is required.
?	A question mark matches exactly zero or one occurrence of the preceding expression. For example, *a?* matches the strings *a* and "" and only those strings.
[ ]	Square brackets are used to designate a character list to be used in matching. For example, regular expression *[0123456789]* matches any single digit, and *[abcdefghijklmnopqrstuvwxyz]* will match any lowercase letter. Within a character list, the following additional special characters can also be used: - The dash indicates a range of matching character values. For example, *[0-9]* matches any single digit, and *[a-z]* matches any single lower-case letter. ^ When a caret is the first character in a character list it is interpreted as a negation symbol, which matches any character that is not in the list. For example, *[^abc]* matches any character except for *a*, *b*, or *c*.
\	The backslash is the escape character, which overrides any special meaning associated with the character that follows it. For example, \[is interpreted as a literal *[* (left square bracket) character, not the beginning of a character list. There are a number of special escape sequences that are also recognized, such as \b for a space and \n to represent a new line character.

Scripting + Regular Expressions = Extreme Programming Power

Imagine that you have a large set of minutes from a defunct organization that have been donated to you, and you have discovered that either the OCR process or the editing operators have inadvertently caused the organization's founder, named Edmund Smith, to often be identified as "Edster" Smith. The minutes have been arranged in a series of files based on the date of the meeting; for example, "Minutes19861130.txt". Because you have many files to process and you want some flexibility with how the files can be handled, you will use the standard input (usually called *stdin*) and standard output (usually called *stdout*) for dealing with the files.

If you haven't heard of stdin and stdout, chances are that you have probably used them at some time on a computer. All operating systems have input/output (I/O) facilities, and most have some simple defaults for managing input/output. There are typically three default I/O options: standard input or stdin, standard output or stdout, and standard error or stderr. We won't worry about standard error at this point, but standard input and standard output are what you interact with in your DOS or command console in Windows operating systems and in any terminal emulation in a UNIX/Linux environment. Modern graphical operating systems have tended to shield users from the oft-termed "command prompt", which is the typical interface to stdin and stdout, but a high comfort level with the command prompt is usually a key ingredient in processing content with scripting tools.

You will see stdin and stdout in action with your scripts, the first of which is constructed in Perl.

```
#read standard input
@lines = <STDIN>;
#look at each line
foreach $line (@lines) {
    #use Regular Expression for making the desired change
    $line =~ s/Edster/Edmund/gi;
    #print the results
    print $line;
}
```

Not surprisingly, Perl is well acquainted with stdin and knows immediately by the "<>" characters that you want to work with content line by line. Perl and most scripting languages can read an entire file in one shot, but working with lines is usually a better idea since a large file can stretch a system's memory resources to the limit. This is the purpose of the *foreach* statement, Perl knows that we want to look at each line individually. The "gi" option in the regular expression statement tells Perl to look for all occurrences—and not to worry about whether the characters are in upper- or lowercase—so that "EDSTER" will become "EDMUND." By default in almost any scripting language, any print or other type of statement that produces output writes to stdout unless told otherwise. Assume that we have put the preceding program in a file called *test* and will run the program from the command prompt as shown:

```
perl test < minutes19861130.txt
ANNUAL MEETING MINUTES
May 3, 1901
...
perl test < minutes19861130.txt > minutes19861130new.txt
```

You can specify the path to the Perl interpreter in Test to avoid typing *perl* in each command, but this will vary depending on platform and where Perl is installed. The "<" and ">" characters are used for redirecting the output of the program. You can see how using stdin and stdout can turn out to be quite useful for processing files: you do not have to edit the program to use as many variations of file names as you want. In the preceding example, you have redirected the contents of the Minutes19861130.txt file into the program with the "<" character, and you have created a modified file called Minutes19861130new.txt with the ">" character. Think of these characters as arrows pointing to where you want content to arrive. Table 8.2 shows how you can take advantage of stdin and stdout to mix and match files for processing.

Table 8.2. Stdin and Stdout in Action.

Objective (*prog* representing our program)	Command
Send *stdout* to *file*	*prog* > file
Take *stdin* from *file*	*prog* < file
Send *stdout* to end of *file* (append)	*prog* > >file

PHP and Python, like most scripting languages outside of Perl, use specific functions to support regular expressions. In the case of PHP, the function *eregi_replace* accomplishes the same results as the "gi" in the Perl example, while Python uses *regsub.gsub*. PHP can be used from the command line, but it is rarely installed that way. More commonly, PHP is built into Apache, and for sheer text processing, it is hard to argue with those who maintain that Perl is the most elegant solution for dealing with text. However, PHP gains a slight edge if you are working in a Web environment. Suppose, for example, that you want to put the results on a Web page, but in this case you are working with a specific file. The following program would accomplish this task within a self-contained HTML page:

```
<HTML>
<HEAD>
<TITLE>Digital Collections at My Library</TITLE>
</HEAD>
<BODY>
<H1>Edmund is not Edster</H1>
<?php
#open the file
$in = fopen("minutes19861130.txt","r") ;
#keep going until the "end of file" (feof) occurs
while (!feof($in)) {
    #get the line
    $line = fgets($in);
    #make the change
    $line = eregi_replace("Edster","Edmund",$line);
    #print it out
    print $line;
    #print the HTML break tag so everything is not on one line
    print "<br/>";
}
?>
</BODY>
</HTML>
```

The edge here is only slight because Perl is also quite Web-savvy, and many would argue, with good reason, that mixing script processing with HTML is a bad idea in the long term for maintenance. Still, for a quick solution, the PHP approach is both workable and Web-friendly.

If you are starting from scratch and have need for only a few scripts to get your collection up and running, Perl may be the easiest option. PHP might make more sense if you plan to have a Web interface and want to use the same language for all of the tools for your digital library. Python, arguably, has the best syntax for multiple maintainers. If you plan to have several hands in the mix for stirring up content, then Python's clean layout and good suitability for large projects may be the best choice. If you already have expertise or good access to expertise with one of these environments over the other, you really can't go wrong with any of them.

A Final Word about XML

What? More about XML! Yes, even when discussing scripting languages for digital libraries, XML is never far away. Almost every scripting language now has tools for XML, and the ones here have entire books devoted to describing how to process XML with them. XML and scripting is a powerful combination and promotes activities such as these:

- Converting text files into XML files

- Changing the contents of large numbers of XML files
- Validating the XML structure of large numbers of files
- Augmenting the contents of XML files with other content

Scripting languages are great for working with a large amount of content that would be cumbersome to do with an XML editor or other tool that is geared for manipulating the contents of one file at a time. Despite the many advantages of an XML-based collection, scripting languages can fill a critical gap if you require frequent or large-scale manipulation of the content of the collection.

Putting It All Together

Scripting languages offer a low-barrier entry point to automating tasks associated with digital libraries. They are particularly well-suited to creating Web applications, processing text, and working with XML. Almost all scripting languages have grown up in the era of the Web, and there are numerous resources for learning about the ones described here, as well as others that combine features from each or take a similar approach. In each case, the goal is usually the same: to offer an environment in which computers can be instructed to perform useful work for the task at hand. By virtue of living in digital space, digital libraries often have need of such services.

9 Plugging Digital Libraries into the Mainstream

Digital libraries, like physical libraries, rarely stand alone. Few other organizations on earth can boast the number of cooperative initiatives that libraries have spearheaded. InterLibrary Loan, joint purchase and licensing agreements, even OCLC, the biggest consortium in the world, are all examples of libraries working together to improve and extend services. Early digital libraries have been characterized as "skunk-works," largely individual and somewhat insular projects that are now expected to join the mainstream, a trend summed up by the description "the maturing digital library."[1]

Some of the earliest and largest digital library projects recognized that solutions for sharing underlying DL technologies were a natural fit for a library environment. For example, in the mid-1990s, the University of Michigan Digital Library Project experimented with software agents to distribute DL functions, and it now offers the Digital Library Extension Service (DLXS) that features both open source tools and a commercial search engine.[2] Stanford's InfoBus project adopted a Java-based technology called Remote Method Invocation (RMI) to "invoke" DL services from distributed systems, and the Stanford Digital Library group developed Simple Digital Library Interoperability Protocol (SDLIP) for defining interactions with distributed DL systems. This work has now been incorporated into SDARTS at Columbia University. SDARTS unites SDLIP with another protocol from Stanford called the Stanford Proposal for Internet Meta-Searching (STARTS) to provide a comprehensive meta-searching protocol.[3]

Finally, as we saw with dlbox, Virginia Tech has done a lot of work with mapping networks of digital libraries as open archives, where individual DLs can provide services in addition to data and participate in a working partnership called OCKHAM, which seeks to make digital library technologies available in an easily deployable fashion.[4]

These approaches fit with a general trend in computer science called componentization, or component-based application building. Components are much like building blocks (see Figure 9.1), reusable pieces of software that can be brought together through a well-defined interface. The implementation of the component should be hidden as much as possible to allow the component to be replaced with another that will retain the same interface. This frees the component developer to utilize different tool sets and encourages best-of-breed component building.

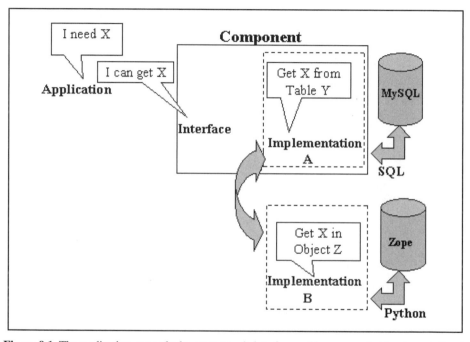

Figure 9.1. The application sees only the component's interface and is unaware that implementation A is about to become implementation B. Note that the implementation can change without changing the storage mechanism, so if X is moved to another table in MySQL, this also can be hidden to the application. In this case, X may be the title of an image or a description of a video clip.

The concept of components is well established in many engineering disciplines, and components make up devices we interact with everyday, such as mobile phones, automobiles, and computers. When a new PC is released by a major manufacturer such as Dell, only a few of the parts have new part numbers, and there are published interfaces for almost all of the internal systems, such as the motherboard and chips. In some cases, these are controlled by one organization or company, but the vast majority are industry standards.

Loosely Coupled versus Highly Coupled

A key aspect of components concerns how independent they are, and components are often characterized as *loosely coupled* or *tightly coupled* to the application to which they are connected. As the names imply, loosely coupled systems are generally less dependent on another application than tightly coupled systems. Many Web applications are considered loosely coupled because they use HTTP to tie different parts of the system together, and even in the most well-maintained network, they are subject somewhat to the ebb and flow of Web throughput.

A simple example that illustrates the concept of a loosely coupled system that will be instantly familiar to any Web designer is the use of the <img> tag to specify an image, such as the following:

```
<img src="/images/dl.jpg">
```

In this case, the target system, that is, the Web browser, interprets this tag to mean, "go to the host site and issue an HTTP request for the image specified by /images/dl.jpg." If the Web server can't find this image or respond to the request, the browser does not stop but continues working with the rest of the content.

Tightly coupled components, on the other hand, are more hardwired into an application. They typically require an *application-level* protocol, in which the semantics of the application are specified directly in the protocol, as opposed to a *transport* protocol such as HTTP. Applications that use tightly coupled components are usually much less forgiving if the component can't deliver what is expected of it. Banking systems and many other applications that require a high level of transaction tracking are more likely to be constructed as tightly coupled systems; they usually have complete control over the components they use, and they are typically housed on one server and share content in the computer's memory rather than over a network connection.

For plugging digital libraries into other systems, the loosely coupled approach normally is acceptable and preferable. Loosely coupled systems allow more autonomy to the participating components and fit well within a distributed Web environment. Any kind of component, though, can work only if it shares a mechanism for finding others and maintains a common agreement for specifying the information to be passed back and forth; this is sometimes called a *component model*.

The Common Object Request Broker Architecture (CORBA),[5] defined by the Object Management Group (OMG), and the Enterprise JavaBeans (EJB)[6] specification from Sun Microsystems are well-known component models that define highly refined interactions between components and excel for putting together component-based systems that require close interactions. Although CORBA and EJB may be good candidates to put together a digital library system on its own, interconnected DL applications and connections between DLs and non-DL systems can normally be defined with component models that have less stringent requirements for participation. Component models such as CORBA and EJB often necessitate that specific software tools be deployed for implementations, a somewhat difficult situation when dealing with systems from other organizations.

An alternative component model, and the one that is described here, is to connect components through XML. This not only allows systems built with such component models as CORBA and EJB to participate, but it also provides a low barrier to adoption for systems that must be retrofitted for component capabilities. Even here, the options are varied and subject to some debate.

XML Integration of Components Using REST and Web Services

Representational State Transfer (REST) is a phrase coined by Roy Fielding, co-founder and director of the Apache Software Foundation. REST is an approach for getting information content from a Web site by reading a designated Web page that contains an XML file that describes and/or includes the desired content. Like the Web, REST is deceptively simple. It relies on HTTP, which, as we saw in Chapter 2, is a straightforward protocol that lends itself to complex network realities, such as firewalls, caching servers, and proxies. REST is firmly based on the notion that URIs and URLs identify network resources and that representations of these resources are delivered across the Web with HTTP. In some ways, URLs represent the ultimate in loosely coupled systems. You can pass a URL from one "system" to another using word of mouth (think of a broadcaster who reads out a URL at the end of a newscast) or even by writing a URL on a piece of paper and handing it to someone else. URLs also do not declare what can or should be done with the information they reference. RSS, OAI, and other protocols that use a URI to retrieve an XML document are utilizing REST. If you type the following URL:

```
http://localhost/content.xml
```

into a browser, you are using REST. Although it is easy to think of HTTP as a largely browser-based technology, there are many toolkits for utilizing HTTP directly from within applications, including ones designed for the scripting languages examined in the last chapter. As a result, REST is sometimes preferred by programmers in addition to those typing URLs in their browsers because it does not require an XML file to be assembled in order to get an XML response.

REST is sometimes described as "XML plus HTTP" and is often pitted against a more extensive set of technologies called Web services (WS), which might be described as "XML plus (HTTP or other) plus XML-RPC or SOAP plus WSDL plus UDDI." These acronyms are explained in some detail later, but an initial way to view Web services is as an option when REST is not enough for getting a digital library to talk to other systems. Despite the current hype behind Web services, don't underestimate the power of REST—it provides significant power for viewing services as collections of components and may be more than adequate for pulling disparate systems together.

We examined SOAP in Chapter 2, but it is worth noting that SOAP was originally intended to be a cross-Internet form of CORBA. XML-Remote Procedure Call (XML-RPC) predates SOAP but is a similar technology for asking a remote computer to perform a task that is specified in XML and receiving the results in XML. If you consider that the central notion of REST is a URL or URI as a pointer to a resource, XML-RPC and SOAP are much more firmly based on the notion of a component residing at the other end of a network connection.

XML-RPC is simpler than SOAP. Recall from Chapter 2 that a SOAP message consists of a header, a body, and an *envelope.* The latter encapsulates the message and annotates it with a form of metadata, such as a reference to the message-encoding specification used to format the message's header and body. In addition to simple data items, SOAP messages may include processing directives. For instance, a SOAP message's intended receiver might advertise a public interface with a method `getLatestAddition()` that can receive a defined material type, such as diary or leaflet, and produces information about the latest item to be added to the collection. A SOAP request using HTTP might look like this:

```
POST /LatestAddition HTTP/1.1
Host: dl.somewhere.org
Content-Type: text/xml;
Charset="utf-8"
Content-Length: 305
SOAPAction: "http://dl.somewhere.org/collection/additions"

<SOAP-ENV:Envelope
    xmlns:SOAP-ENV="http://www.w3c.org/2001/12/soap-envelope"
    SOAP-ENV:encodingStyle="http://schemas.xmlsoap.org/soap/encoding"/>
        <SOAP-ENV:Body>
            <m:getLatestAddition
                xmlns:m="http://dl.somewhere.org/collection/additions"
                <additionType>Leaflet
                </additionType>
            </m:getLatestAddition>
        </SOAP-ENV:Body>
</SOAP-ENV:Envelope>
```

Compare this to an equivalent XML-RPC request:

```
POST /LatestAddition HTTP/1.1
Host: dl.somewhere.org
Content-Type: text/xml;
Charset="utf-8"
Content-Length: 178
```

```
<?xml version="1.0"?>
<methodCall>
        <methodName>getLatestEdition</methodName>
        <params>
            <parm>
                    <additionType>Leaflet</additionType>
            </parm>
        </params>
</methodCall>
```

As you can see, the SOAP is more verbose than REST and XML-RPC, and usually requires additional software to package requests, unless you are extremely fond of coding XML by hand. The response in either case looks quite similar structurally to the request. For example, using SOAP, it looks like this:

```
HTTP/1.1 200 OK Content-Type: text/xml; charset="utf-8"
Content-Length: 357

<SOAP-ENV:Envelope
    xmlns:SOAP-ENV="http://www.w3c.org/2001/12/soap-envelope"
    SOAP-ENV:encodingStyle="http://schemas.xmlsoap.org/soap/encoding"/>
        <SOAP-ENV:Body>
            <m:getLatestAdditionResponse
                xmlns:m="http://dl.somewhere.org/collection/additions"
                <addition>Robert Frost's First Impressions of the North
                </addition>
            </m:getLatestAdditionResponse>
        </SOAP-ENV:Body>
</SOAP-ENV:Envelope>
```

On its own, an XML-RPC or SOAP request or response is just another XML document. SOAP has additional capabilities that add value to component interactions, such as the ability to add digital signatures to the header section, and implementations can process multiple messages in one document. But where Web services really start to differ from REST approaches is through yet another XML document. This document describes the component's interface in a syntax known as the Web Service Description Language (WSDL).

Understanding WSDL

If SOAP messages are verbose, WSDL documents can be excruciatingly detailed. WSDL contains a set of definitions that describe a Web service and should normally provide all of the information needed to access and use the service. In general, you would use a toolkit to generate WSDL for a Web service, and the results might resemble the following:

```
<?xml version="1.0"?>
<definitions name="LatestAddition"
        targetNameSpace="http://dl.somewhere.org/latestaddtion.wsdl"
        xmlns:tns="http://dl.somewhere.org/latestaddition.wsdl"
        xmlns:xsd="http://www.w3.org/2001/XMLSchema"
        xmlns:soap="http://schemas.xmlsoap.org/wsdl/soap/"
        xmlns="http://schemas.xmlsoap.org/wsdl">

<documentation>
 WSDL service interface definition for a Digital Library latest addition service.
</documentation>

<message name="getLatestAdditionRequest">
 <part name="additionType" type="xsd:string"/>
</message>
<message name="getLatestAdditionResponse">
 <part name="addition" element="xsd:string"/>
</message>

<portType name="LatestAdditionService">
 <operation name="getLatestAddition">
  <input message="tns:getLatestAdditionRequest"/>
  <output message="tns:getLatestAdditionResponse"/>
 </operation>
</portType>

<binding name="LatestAdditionBinding"
        type="tns:LatestAdditionService">
 <soap:binding style="document"
  transport="http://schemas.xmlsoap.org/soap/http"/>
 <operation name="getLatestAddition">
  <soap:operation soapAction="http://dl.somewhere.org/collection/additions"/>
   <input>
    <soap:body use="encoded"
     namespace="urn:addition-types"
     encodingStyle="http://schemas.xmlsoap.org/soap/encoding/"/>
   </input>
   <output>
    <soap:body use="encoded"
     encodingStyle="http://schemas.xmlsoap.org/soap/encoding/"/>
   </output>
  </operation>
 </binding>
</definitions>
```

The definitions element starts by naming the WSDL document (http://dl.somewhere.org/latestaddtion.wsdl) and specifies the namespaces that will be needed for the Web service. The documentation element briefly describes the Web service and defines a message that is an abstract definition of what will be accepted and produced by the service. The portType and operation elements define the operations that will be carried out, so that a getLatestAdditionRequest will invoke a getLatestAdditionResponse, and the binding element specifies how you will receive the response. The style attribute can specify rpc or document. With rpc, the response will be received with the XML element (<?xml version="1.0"?>) at the top. Specifying document causes the response to omit this. The transport attribute specifies the network protocol, in this case HTTP, that will be used. Finally, the `input` and `output` elements designate how the request or response will be marked up or `encoded` for the service.

The level of detail in WSDL allows for a great amount of precision in defining what a service will support and the types of interactions it supports. For example, the WSDL document can tie the data that comes from an application to an XML Schema so that only specific values are allowed. This could be used to ensure that only the latest additions for materials that are defined as diaries, photographs, or leaflets can be requested.

WSDL is not limited to SOAP or XML-RPC; it also can be used to specify REST services, though in practice WSDL has been used almost exclusively for SOAP interactions. Where WSDL may have its greatest value is in graphical application development environments. By using a WSDL file, a developer might get a visual rendering of the list of services that are available and which parameters are acceptable; for example, in a drop-down list. This is a key part of the debate between REST and Web services: stuffing parameters in a URL may be a preferred approach if no development environment is available or for tying applications together quickly, but a fully loaded development environment may be far more amenable to using WSDL.

Like many Web debates, REST versus SOAP is really a trade-off between the infrastructure and preferences of the participants. A latest-addition service like the one in the examples could easily fit into either REST or Web services. On the other hand, a latest-addition service requiring digital signatures or an extensive number of parameters to be passed back and forth would probably be better deployed using Web services and the capabilities of WSDL.

A Quick Look at UDDI

The final piece of Web services is called Universal Description, Discovery, and Integration (UDDI). UDDI resembles a yellow pages service: you create an entry for your organization, specifying your organization's name, and then define which Web services your organization offers, how to access those Web services, and which specifications those services implement, typically by linking to the WSDL description of the service. You can see how UDDI fits into the picture in Figure 9.2.

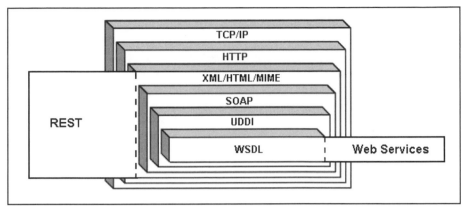

Figure 9.2. UDDI sits a layer above WSDL and helps a client identify a needed Web service.

UDDI is a registry-based system, and so far at least, all of the existing UDDI registries are free of charge for using and adding entries. Despite this, the bulk of the effort with UDDI has largely been slanted toward e-commerce and business applications. Currently, IBM and Microsoft, as well as a few others, offer UDDI registries. One interesting aspect of UDDI is that no matter which registry instance you go to, the registry provider should synchronize registration information with others, and UDDI is somewhat comparable to the Domain Name System (DNS). This means that the same service descriptions normally are available in all registries. UDDI uses taxonomies for classifying services, and the most common deployment is the North American Industry Classification System (NAICS).[7]

It is possible to add alternatives to NAICS and use them with others, but there is a registration process that must involve the UDDI operator if the taxonomy is to be made available to everyone. Key concepts in UDDI include that of a *tModel,* which specifies the protocol and other information about the connection, and checked and unchecked taxonomies. A *checked* taxonomy is one in which users must use the classification entries to find services; an *unchecked* UDDI taxonomy is one that does not enforce this requirement. An example UDDI entry, in an unchecked taxonomy, looks like this:

```
<tModel authorizedName="..." operator="..."
 tModelKey="uuid:11111111-2222-3333-4444-555555555555">
 <name>dl:partner_types</name>
 <overviewDoc>
  <description xml:lang="en">DL taxonomy.
  </description>
  <overviewURL>
   http://dl.somewhere.org/dl_ taxonomy.html
  </overviewURL>
 </overviewDoc>
 <categoryBag>
  <keyedReference
```

```
   tModelKey="uuid:YYY22929YY-0000-1111-2222-9888X9999"
   keyName="uddi-org:types"
   keyValue="categorization"/>
 <keyedReference
   tModelKey=" uuid:YY22298XX-0000-1111-2222-9888XSSS8"
   keyName="uddi-org:types"
   keyValue="unchecked"/>
 </categoryBag>
</tModel>
```

Because UDDI is a registry technology, it focuses on universally unique identifier (UUID) *keys,* which uniquely identify the service, so that *uuid: YYY22929YY-0000-1111-2222-9888X9999,* for example, is not confused with other Web services.

At this point, UDDI is probably more in the "technologies to watch" category for digital libraries than it is a type of system that will have an immediate impact on DL applications. UDDI and an appropriate taxonomy might eventually be a great value for resource discovery if DL Web services become widely available. Work to unite Semantic Web technology with UDDI may prove to be a promising means of automatically identifying Web services.[8]

Cocoon and XSLT as Component Equalizers

The REST/SOAP/Web services debates are interesting from an academic point of view, but the reality is that you may not have any choice about how a service is made available. Google, for example, uses SOAP for accessing such services as the "did you mean?" term engine, and many mainstream toolkits for technologies as varied as Grid computing and textual analysis also build on a Web services infrastructure. Digital libraries implemented with OAI tools are more likely to use REST, though some DL systems, such as Fedora, support REST and Web services approaches. The trend in digital library applications seems to be moving toward having options for both.

In general, mechanisms that can leverage both REST or Web services options for a remote service tend to come in handy for augmenting a digital library with additional services. One compelling option that brings together components with general Web technologies is Cocoon. Recall from Chapter 4 that Cocoon is a Java-based environment that can be run on any machine that has a Java Virtual Machine. Cocoon uses pipelines to produce formats from XML content using components that have been donated to the Apache Foundation. These components are "wired in" to the pipeline using XSLT and a process that involves a generator (which produces SAX events from XML content), a transformer (which applies the XSLT processing), and a serializer (which ensures that the content is passed in the appropriate format).

In Chapter 4, we saw how these sitemaps could be used to deliver different types of content depending on the request; for example, producing a page in Wireless Access Protocol (WAP) format from XML content:

```
<map:match pattern="welcome.wml">
  <map:generate src="rare_manuscripts/welcome.xml"/>
  <map:transform src="stylesheets/page2wml.xsl"/>
  <map:serialize type="wap"/>
</map:match>
```

With Cocoon, it is also possible to use this process to bring together components with either REST or SOAP origins. For example, using the database defined in Chapter 5 with MySQL, you might decide to use Google to identify Web resources relating to selected works in your collection. First, you would define an XML document called Query.xml that will take advantage of a component called the SQL Transformer that comes with Cocoon:

```
<artist-list>
  <sql:execute-query>
    <sql:query>
      SELECT work_title FROM works WHERE id = <xsp-request:get-
parameter id="id"/>
    </sql: query>
  </sql:execute-query>
</artist-list>
```

Cocoon has sophisticated support for databases, particularly relational databases, that helps maximize throughput using such techniques as connection pooling, in which the system maintains a set of connections to a database so that an application does not have to wait for a new one to be constructed for each request. It is not necessary to know this level of detail when using Cocoon, but this kind of support can be critical for a busy Web site. The output from the SQL Transformer is, naturally, in XML and looks like the following:

```
<row-set>
  <row>
    <title_parm>Brown Wolf</title_parm>
  </row>
</row-set>
```

Using an XSLT file called Authors-for-google.xsl, you can change this output to a format Google's Web services implementation expects. The SOAP request for Google consists of the following XML statements:

```
<soap:query url="http://www.google.com:8089">
 <?xml version="1.0" encoding="UTF-8"?>
<xsp:page
  language="java"
  xmlns:xsp="http://apache.org/xsp"
  xmlns:xsp-request="http://apache.org/xsp/request/2.0"
  xmlns:soap="http://apache.org/xsp/soap/3.0"
  >
```

```
<search-results>
  <soap:call url="http://api.google.com:80/search/beta2"
      xmlns:xsi="http://www.w3.org/1999/XMLSchema-instance"
      xmlns:xsd="http://www.w3.org/1999/XMLSchema">
    <ns1:doGoogleSearch xmlns:ns1="urn:GoogleSearch">
      <key xsi:type="xsd:string">GOOGLEKEY</key>
      <q xsi:type="xsd:string">Brown Wolf</q>
      <start xsi:type="xsd:int">0</start>
      <maxResults xsi:type="xsd:int">10</maxResults>
      <filter xsi:type="xsd:boolean">true</filter>
      <restrict xsi:type="xsd:string"></restrict>
      <safeSearch xsi:type="xsd:boolean">false</safeSearch>
      <lr xsi:type="xsd:string"></lr>
      <ie xsi:type="xsd:string">latin1</ie>
      <oe xsi:type="xsd:string">latin1</oe>
    </ns1:doGoogleSearch>
  </soap:call>
</search-results>
</xsp:page>
</soap:query>
```

Note that the GOOGLEKEY is actually a long numeric string that has to come from Google and is supplied when you register with Google to use Web services. Typical of SOAP messages, the XML is quite verbose, but these options are also what you set or tacitly accept when you use Google through a browser. With many Web services, every option is brought forward to the SOAP messages that flow back and forth.

The pipelines are assembled in the sitemap, which looks like the following:

```
<!—Sitemap Entry for SQL work->
<map:match ="sqlworks">
  <map:act type="request">
    <map:generate src="query.xml"/>
    <map:transformer type="sql">
      <map:parameter name="use-connection" value="dl"/>
    </map:transformer>
    <map:parameter name="parameters" value="true"/>
    <map:transformer type="xsl" src="Authors-for-google.xsl"/>
  </map:act>
</map:match>

<!—Sitemap Entry for SOAP->
<map:match="googlecheck">
  <map:act type="request">
    <map:generate
        type="serverpages" src="cocoon:/sqlworks?id={id}"/>
    <map:parameter name="parameters" value="true"/>
    <map:transformer type="xsl" src="html-out.xsl"/>
    <map:serialize type="html"/>
  </map:act>
</map:match>
```

The sitemap uses Cocoon's own protocol with the *cocoon:/* designation to pull in the output from the SQL section. Note that the XSLT file "html-out.xsl" changes the XML output from Google to the HTML format to be delivered to the user's browser. Any number of services can be brought together in the pipeline, with XSLT providing the mechanism to change the XML output of one into the format expected of the other.

Cocoon provides a way to share common infrastructure between digital libraries and other Web resources. If Cocoon and XSLT can be thought of as equalizers in utilizing both REST and Web services for digital library applications, the sitemap can be thought of as a form of "component glue," enabling the reuse of components across a Web landscape and delivering content in whatever format makes the most sense for the user community.

Putting It All Together

Web services are a compelling architecture for building digital library services out of components and utilizing third-party applications. Much of the plumbing for Web services requires some intense XML, but so many mainstream technologies now are built with Web services that it is expected that toolkits will become common. Cocoon is one possible infrastructure for bringing together XML-based components regardless of whether they are based on REST or SOAP.

10 Long-Term Care and Feeding of Digital Libraries

So, you have built your digital library—what comes next? Sorry to say, but this is just the beginning of the process. Libraries are typically starting points for many intellectual journeys; it is a rare resource that meets every conceivable need of all those who use it. Digital library systems represent an important first step in providing services for a community, but like physical libraries, digital libraries will evolve and require generous attention along the way.

The Digital Library as Place and Space

Libraries are wondrous spaces, in addition to the richness of the content in the library's collection, libraries often provide an extensive physical infrastructure for working with the materials they house, from desks to printers, pencil sharpeners to PCs. A digital library may enable access to materials that can use a wide variety of associated tools. The Perseus Digital Library,[1] for example, uses Virtual Reality Markup Language (VRML)[2] and other 3D tools to offer an immersive experience of the era or location of the collection documents (see Figure 10.1). A sound collection may be well served by having links to audio analysis applications, and the many digital libraries that feature access to text might round out the collection with selected visual tools such as images that capture the architecture of the time that the collection was authored.

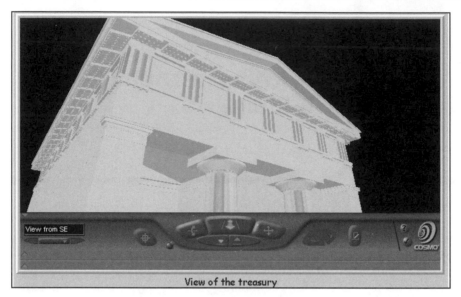

View from SE

View of the treasury

Figure 10.1. A VRML model from Perseus.

Digital libraries that can offer users virtual space to collect and organize materials from the collection will be able to provide a sometimes much-needed option to manage digital information. A desk in a library frequently is a gathering point for mounds of open books and journals for both the serious researcher and a library user browsing multiple items. Personal and collaborative systems that can be used as a storage or work area in a user's digital travels may help maximize the benefits of a virtual collection.

Open source software has many options for building systems that can provide a place to gather content for personal use and for group-level collaboration. MyLibrary,[3] Zope's Content Management Framework (CMF)[4] portal and blogging systems, uPortal,[5] and many other OSS applications are available for doing the virtual equivalent of adding the desks and the chairs to go with the stacks and the books in a physical library. The digital library might also be an opportunity to try out innovative programs that might be difficult or impossible in a physical setting. For example, "commonplace" books were used for centuries for patrons to write down memorable thoughts and musings; a DL would be a good location to offer facilities for an online community to create its own commonplace publications.

Recent work in the digital library community and by the W3C in annotations would fit in well as part of a DL service.[6] An *annotation* in this sense is a comment made on a Web-based resource. The OSS Annozilla server[7] and associated plug-ins for Web browsers would be an easy method of distributing tools for viewing and creating annotations (see Figure 10.2) for a digital collection. The CYCLADES[8] system is an example of an application that incorporates sophisticated annotation features directly within a digital library.

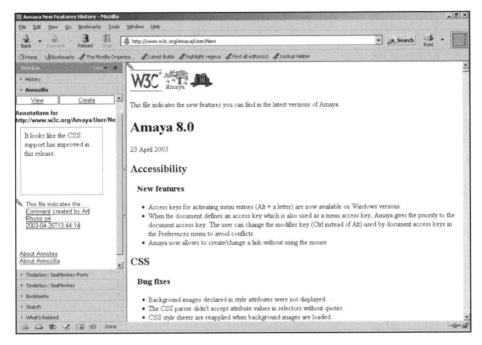

Figure 10.2. Annotations in action. Here, an annotation is loaded automatically when a Web page is retrieved. This same approach could be used, for example, within a community of scholars when viewing digital objects.

Digital library systems can produce XML easily and, assuming sufficient granularity, may be linked to numerous applications. For example, a URL could provide an XML list of all the works by a certain historical figure. XPointer allows sections of XML documents to be specified, opening the door to referencing portions of a document in other contexts. Librarians know that the content of the materials they make available will be used in all kinds of contexts, but there will always be uses that no one foresees. A digital library that allows its resources to be linked to anything stands a better chance of being actively used in other environments.

Some digital library implementations support the notion of a persistent ID for a digital object; for example, Fedora has a persistent identifier (PID) and DSpace uses the CNRI Handle system to construct a permanent URL to an entry. It also may be possible to construct a URL that will retrieve the same digital object repeatedly using some well-defined criterion. In either case, enabling digital objects to be referenced consistently from external systems is an important step in allowing the object to be plugged into bookmark organizers, portals, and other types of tools for managing digital content.

Preserving and Future-Proofing Collections

Preservation has been called a time bomb for digital libraries. Jeff Rothenberg has compared digital content to "invisible ink"[9] because such content has been written in the language of machines and requires the right machine resources to render it just as materials using invisible ink require the appropriate solvent. At least five general approaches have been proposed for digital preservation:

1. Migration. Periodic updating or rewriting of old data to run on new configurations/platforms.

2. Emulation. Mimicking older platforms so that the operating environment for obsolete software and data files can be recreated.

3. Encapsulation. Providing digital objects with instructions on how to re-create the platform needed to enable their use.

4. Multiple strategic backups. Making copies of content in formats that stand a good chance of being reconstructed, such as image formats, in which there is a one-to-one correspondence between how coordinates are stored and displayed, and paper or other physical renderings that capture the content and have a track record for long-term storage, as well as placing copies in as many locations as possible.

5. Universal decoding. Relying on a set of widely promulgated and machine-independent applications that could unlock files and run application software at any time in the future. As content is created, a copy would be saved in a format that could be decoded.

Of course, the solutions are time-bound as well, since there is no guarantee that any digital entity can be resuscitated in the future. Preservation is at best a commitment to try to do as much as possible to ensure future generations will be able to use content created today.

The good news is that preservation has become a widely recognized problem, mainly because digital content has been around long enough for preservation issues to have garnered the spotlight. For example, there is satellite data from the 1970s that would be useful for understanding global warning that is currently unreadable. Governments and other large organizations are starting to recognize the costs and implications of not being able to retrieve records from the past few decades. As noted in *Digital Libraries: Universal Access to Human Knowledge* (President's Information Technology Advisory Committee), each new medium seems to deteriorate more rapidly than its predecessor: "We can still read illuminated manuscripts created in the 12th century, but within a few decades a file stored several years ago on an eight-inch floppy disk may be lost forever."[10]

There are a number of steps that can be taken to help "future-proof" a digital collection. A common refrain in the digital library field is "when in doubt, use ASCII." A variation of this would be to use Unicode and XML, with a well-recognized schema. XML content is nonproprietary and stands a good chance of being discernable in the future. It also can be printed and saved on paper and other nonelectronic formats.

Be aware of XML solutions that produce or read XML but don't use XML as an internal format. XML is verbose and there are solid technical reasons for an application not to use it internally, but get into the habit of saving copies of all content in XML proper. OSS applications have the huge advantage over proprietary systems that the source code is available if it were necessary to reconstruct the environment in which certain content was created, but it is important to realize that modern platforms have so many interdependencies that total reconstruction may be unrealistic.

One easy step to make for preserving digital collections is to make lots of copies. Disk space has become very cheap and the Internet has created a global conduit for placing copies in other regions and systems. Stanford University and Sun Microsystems have created a peer-to-peer system called Lots of Copies Keep Stuff Safe (LOCKSS)[11] that is available with a BSD-like license and runs on Java so that it can conceivably be deployed on almost any platform. You might also consider exposing your content as a series of HTML files to be picked up by Internet search engines. For example, DP9[12] creates a series of HTML files for an OAI repository. This places the digital library's content into the caches of Internet search engines and systems such as the Internet Wayback Machine,[13] an archive of the World Wide Web's past.

The Reference Model for an Open Archival Information System (OAIS)

The OAIS reference model[14] was released in May 1999 by the Consultative Committee for Space Data Systems (CCSDS), an international collaboration of space agencies that had been requested by the International Organisation for Standardization (ISO) to develop a stand for the long-term storage of digital data. With OAIS, the goal is to assign meaning to the stream of bits that make up a digital object in order to create an information object. An *information object* is a digital object combined with the representational information to provide the structural and semantic information required to understand the object. For example, structural information might indicate a bit stream as ASCII text, while the semantic information might indicate the language is English. In other words, OAIS focuses on preserving the bit stream and the information surrounding it rather than the media on which it is contained.

OAIS uses the concept of information packages, which describe objects at different points in the archive. A *submission information package* (SIP) is defined as the objects sent to the archive by the information producer, an *archive information package* (AIP) is the grouping of objects that is actually stored by the system, and the *dissemination information package* (DIP) represents the objects that are presented to the user for a request (see Figure 10.3).

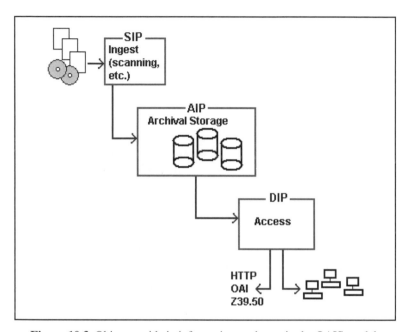

Figure 10.3. Objects reside in information packages in the OAIS model.

OAIS lays out the processes seen in the figure. For example, *ingest* refers to the process of separating the record from its media to a more standard file format, and *archival storage* is the process of storing the record. OAIS defines other processes associated with each information package, such as *administration* for running the archive, which involves far more detail than can be sketched here. Reference models are conceptual models that provide a basis for creating functioning systems, and you may see reference to information packages, especially to the AIP, when reading the documentation of digital library applications or, even more likely, when reading reports on digital library projects.

Prototypes of the OAIS model also have been built as part of the CURL Exemplars in Digital Archives (Cedars)[15] and other preservation projects. OAIS is probably the most recognized international standard for preservation, and it is a key building block for defining a preservation strategy. It is a model that is well worth becoming familiar with as you evaluate OSS systems or investigate digital library projects to plan for preservation early in the process.

Project Proposals and Reports

One of the most useful documents ever put together for building digital libraries is the Institute of Museum and Library Services's (IMLS's) *Framework for Building Good Digital Collections.*[16] The framework includes a projects section that identifies three principles:

1. A good project has a substantial design component.

2. A good project has an evaluation plan.

3. A good project produces a project report.

An underlying theme behind these principles is planning. Getting a collection online is arguably not that hard with many of the tools identified in this book. Putting a sustainable collection and service together is much more difficult. It has been noted that migration and similar preservation strategies are rarely written into project proposals,[17] but this is exactly where the groundwork for preservation should occur. Preservation invariably requires effort and resources, and these issues should be identified early in the process.

Open source software depends on a community to share code, but the open source philosophy is fundamentally about sharing in general. Creating and sharing information about a digital library project, especially through a project report that gives a frank assessment of what practices and methodologies were helpful and describes what lessons were learned in the process, is an excellent way to help others put together projects.

A step as simple as putting a link to a report on the front page of a digital collection will help others make informed choices, particularly when the organization is small and the viewed collection has been assembled by a comparably sized institution.

Measuring Use and Soliciting User Feedback

Libraries of all types tend to be service organizations. The vast resources found in a library are dependent on an infrastructure that requires significant human interaction to fulfill the needs of the community. All service organizations need to gauge how well they are accomplishing their task and maintain an evolving sense of their users' needs.

Digital libraries are no exception. Normally, usage statistics can be accumulated easily on the basis of Web-related tools such as hit counters and Web-log analysis. Direct user feedback can be more difficult to obtain but is invaluable for enhancing services and shaping the future growth of the collection. This might take the form of focus groups and other formal activities to draw out information on whether the digital library is accomplishing what its creators hoped for.

Several initiatives to develop appropriate measures for digital collections exist, including the Measures for Electronic Resources project from the Association of Research Libraries, which are identified in the Further Resources section. Organizations that run existing electronic services may have advantages here since they already may have mechanisms in place for measuring use.

Metrics for Success

The range of digital libraries and digital library software, even open source digital library software, is almost as broad as the collections the applications serve. Digital library projects typically evolve with changes in technology and user expectations. The system underlying a digital collection may require modifications or additions that were never conceived of in the planning stages. Here are a few questions to help you get a sense of whether your digital library will be well positioned for future growth:

- How easily can the digital library produce and accept XML content?

- How many steps does it take for you to add a new media type to the collection?

- Users of five different software packages have asked whether they can import some records from your system into their own. Can you meet all of these requests?

- The main creator of the software you use has given up programming and moved to Tahiti to live on a beach. Your boss has just been informed. What is your response?

The Further Resources section is intended to help you tackle these questions and others as they arise. With open standards and software, you stand a good chance of not only finding an answer, but also participating in community-built solutions.

Putting It All Together

Augmenting or adding services to a digital library can make it a more welcoming environment. The use of persistent IDs facilitates plugging content into external systems and increases the likelihood that the content will be referenced from other systems. Digital content also presents unique preservation challenges, and the OAIS reference model represents a major step toward a common framework for preservation. Planning in advance and writing a report at the conclusion of a digital library project helps to create a successful experience both for you and for others who may follow your example, and soliciting feedback from the users of a digital collection will help guide further enhancements. Above all, ask lots of questions, ensure as much flexibility as possible, and build systems that are worthy of their content.

Appendix

The Open Source Definition

Introduction

Open source doesn't just mean access to the source code. The distribution terms of open source software must comply with the following criteria.

1. Free Redistribution

The license shall not restrict any party from selling or giving away the software as a component of an aggregate software distribution containing programs from several different sources. The license shall not require a royalty or other fee for such sale.

2. Source Code

The program must include source code and must allow distribution in source code as well as compiled form. Where some form of a product is not distributed with source code, there must be a well-publicized means of obtaining the source code for no more than a reasonable reproduction cost, preferably downloading via the Internet without charge. The source code must be the preferred form in which a programmer would modify the program. Deliberately obfuscated source code is not allowed. Intermediate forms such as the output of a preprocessor or translator are not allowed.

3. Derived Works

The license must allow modifications and derived works, and must allow them to be distributed under the same terms as the license of the original software.

4. Integrity of the Author's Source Code

The license may restrict source code from being distributed in modified form *only* if the license allows the distribution of "patch files" with the source code for the purpose of modifying the program at build time. The license must explicitly permit distribution of software built from modified source code. The license may require derived works to carry a different name or version number from the original software.

5. No Discrimination against Persons or Groups

The license must not discriminate against any person or group of persons.

6. No Discrimination against Fields of Endeavour

The license must not restrict anyone from making use of the program in a specific field of endeavour. For example, it may not restrict the program from being used in a business or from being used for genetic research.

7. Distribution of License

The rights attached to the program must apply to all to whom the program is redistributed without the need for execution of an additional license by those parties.

8. License Must Not Be Specific to a Product

The rights attached to the program must not depend on the program's being part of a particular software distribution. If the program is extracted from that distribution and used or distributed within the terms of the program's license, all parties to whom the program is redistributed should have the same rights as those that are granted in conjunction with the original software distribution.

9. The License Must Not Restrict Other Software

The license must not place restrictions on other software that is distributed along with the licensed software. For example, the license must not insist that all other programs distributed on the same medium must be open source software.

10. The License Must Be Technology-Neutral

No provision of the license may be predicated on any individual technology or style of interface.

Source: www.opensource.org/docs/definition_plain.php

Notes

Preface

1. librarycog.uwindsor.ca.

Introduction

1. Information about the DLF can be found at www.diglib.org.

2. Widely quoted, but seems to originate in a draft policy document at www.diglib.org/about/strategic.htm.

3. See, for example, the Association of Research Libraries (ARL) definition at www.libnet.sh.cn/diglib/definition.htm.

4. A good starting point for this is David Levy, "Going Digital: A Look at Assumptions Underlying Digital Libraries," *Communications of the ACM* 38, no. 4 (April 1995): 77–84.

5. The OSI site is www.opensource.org/.

6. The most up-to-date version of the definition is maintained at www.opensource.org/docs/definition.php.

7. One of many versions of this can be found at First Monday (1998) at www.firstmonday.dk/issues/issue3_3/raymond/.

8. See GNU Project—The Free Software Definition at www.gnu.org/philosophy/free-sw.html.

9. The study is available at www.infonomics.nl/FLOSS/.

10. Maintained at www.gnu.org/copyleft/gpl.html.

11. See creativecommons.org/learn/licenses/.

12. For example, see Jon Udell's LibraryLookup project at weblog.infoworld.com/udell/stories/2002/12/11/librarylookup.html.

13. Maintained at www.gnu.org/copyleft/lesser.html.

14. The main site is www.perl.com/language/misc/Artistic.html. See also www.opensource.org/licenses/artistic-license.php.

15. The best source is from OSI at www.opensource.org/licenses/bsd-license.php.

16. The latest version of the license is kept at www.apache.org/
     LICENSE.

17. See OSI at www.opensource.org/licenses/mit-license.php.

18. Various locations. The OSI version is at www.opensource.org/licenses/
     UoI-NCSA.php.

19. The starting point for both MPL and NPL is at www.mozilla.org/
     MPL/.

20. See www.mozilla.org/MPL/.

21. Maintained at www.oclc.org/research/software/license/index.shtm.

22. Wendy Pradt Lougee captures the connection between open models
     and libraries in *Diffuse Libraries: Emergent Roles for the Research
     Library in the Digital Age* (Council on Library and Information Re-
     sources, August 2002). Available at www.clir.org/pubs/reports/
     pub108/contents.html.

Chapter 1

1. One estimate is that the world produces between 1 and 2 exabytes (a
    billion billion 8-bit bytes) of information a year, approximately 250
    megabytes for every person on earth.   More than 90 percent of this con-
    tent is stored in digital form and is primarily image, sound, and numeric
    data. Printed documents account for a miniscule 0.003 percent of the to-
    tal. (Source: President's Information Technology Advisory Committee,
    Digital Libraries: Universal Access to Human Knowledge [2001].
    Available at www.ccic.gov/pubs/pitac/pitac-dl-9feb01.pdf.)

2. This is the terminology used in the invaluable *Framework of Guid-
    ance for Building Good Digital Collections* (Institute of Museum and
    Library Services, November 6, 2001). Available at www.imls.gov/
    pubs/forumframework.htm.

3. Ibid.

4. American Standard Code for Information Interchange (ASCII) is a
    code for representing Latin characters as numbers, with each letter as-
    signed a number from 0 to 127. It is not nearly as capable as other en-
    coding schemes but is the most widely supported.

5. Unicode is capable of encoding all known characters and is main-
    tained by the Unicode Consortium, a nonprofit organization.

6. SAS (Statistical Analysis System) is a statistics platform that features
    a programming language for data manipulation and statistical analysis.

7. SPSS (Statistical Package for the Social Sciences) is a statistics platform similar to SAS and also is widely supported.

8. See www.tei-c.org/.

9. The official EAD site is at www.loc.gov/ead/.

10. *Master* refers to the highest-quality versions allowed that preserves the most accurate facsimile. The IMLS framework uses an example of a master copy of a digitally reformatted 35mm slide, which might be an uncompressed, 18-megabyte TIFF file, captured in 24-bit color at a resolution of 600 dots per inch (dpi). See the *IMLS Framework* for examples as well as Kenney's and Rieger's chapters in Anne R. Kenney and Oya Y. Rieger, *Moving Theory into Practice* (Mountain View, Calif.: Research Libraries Group, 2000).

11. These graphic formats are defined in the glossary.

12. MrSID is a proprietary file format and was the first popular wavelet-based compression program to compress extremely large images to a fraction of their original file size without quality loss.

13. JPEG 2000 can't yet match MrSID compression yet and, at the time of this writing, is still not widely supported. But it is an open standard and is starting to be incorporated into applications. See the JPEG Web site at www.jpeg.org/.

14. See the glossary for definitions.

15. Most Internet users are well acquainted with these formats.   See the glossary for more information.

16. Probably the best-known streaming format is RealAudio, marketed by RealNetworks.

17. For more details, see *A Brief History of the Development of SGML* at www.sgmlsource.com/history/sgmlhist.htm.

18. Tim Berners-Lee's book is a fascinating account of the process that led to the use of HTML. See Tim Berners-Lee, and Mark Fischetti, *Weaving the Web: The Original Design and Ultimate Destiny of the World Wide Web by Its Inventor* (San Francisco, Calif.: Harper, 2000).

19. These, and many other, XML standards can be found at the XML Cover Pages (xml.coverpages.org), possibly the most comprehensive collection of XML initiatives available.

20. See Anne J. Gilliland-Swetland, *Introduction to Metadata: Pathways to Digital Information*, version 2, edited by Murtha Baca (Getty Information Institute, 2000). Available at www.getty.edu/research/institute/standards/intrometadata/index.html.

21. The Library of Congress Network Development and MARC Standards Office is the maintainer of the MARC standard, and extensive documentation can be found at www.loc.gov/marc/.

22. See both the Cover Pages entries for XML and MARC at xml.coverpages.org/marc.html, as well as Stanford University's Lane Medical Library XMLMARC site at xmlmarc.stanford.edu/.

23. Like MARC, METS is maintained by the Network Development and MARC Standards Office at the Library of Congress; see www.loc.gov/standards/mets/.

24. This vision may best be exemplified in the May 2001 issue of *Scientific American.* See Tim Berners-Lee, James Hendler, and Ora Lassila, "The Semantic Web," *Scientific American.* Available at www.sciam.com/issue.cfm?issuedate=May-01.

25. If you visited almost any Web service–related newsgroup around the time the May 2001 issue of *Scientific American* came out, you would have encountered lots of hostility directed toward this W3C initiative. Summed up by CNN at news.com.com/2100-1023-834990.html.

26. The W3C site for RDF is www.w3.org/RDF/.

27. See, for example, Tim Bray's work on Resource/Property/Value (RPV) at www.textuality.com/xml/RPV.html.

28. A quick, concise, and easy-to-read introduction to the RDF schema, DAML+OIL can be found at HP Labs, "Introduction to Semantic Web Technologies." Available at www.hpl.hp.com/semweb/sw-technology.htm.

29. The TAP Project page is at tap.stanford.edu/.

30. Topic Maps is not a W3C activity and is maintained by an independent consortium. The Topic Map Specification is, however, licensed to the public. See www.topicmaps.org/xtm/index.html.

31. rdfDB can be found at www.guha.com/rdfdb/.

32. See, for example, the Omnigator at www.ontopia.net/omnigator/models/index.jsp.

33. The Edutella project page is at edutella.jxta.org/.

Chapter 2

1. The W3C Page for HTTP is www.w3.org/Protocols/.

2. TCP/IP in fact uses several protocols, but the two main ones are Transmission Control Protocol (TCP) and Internet Protocol (IP). TCP handles the connection between two systems for general exchanges of data, and IP passes *packets,* predefined units of data, back and forth.

3. See the CNRI Handle site, www.handle.net/.

4. The PURL software and documentation can be found at www.purl.org/.

5. A good starting point for OpenURL is the overview at www.sfxit. com/OpenURL/. At least one OSS implementation of an OpenURL revolver exists; see Andy Powell, "OpenResolver: A Simple OpenURL Resolver," *Adriane* 28 (June 2001). Available at www. ariadne.ac.uk/issue28/resolver/.

6. MIME types are outlined at www.mhonarc.org/~ehood/MIME/ MIME.html.

7. This was a background paper, and it can be viewed at www. w3.org/ HTandCERN.txt. The main paper was entitled *Information Management,* and it is available at www.w3.org/History/1989/proposal. html.

8. See the Apache History Project—Timelime at www.apache.org/ history/timeline.html.

9. About page at httpd.apache.org/ABOUT_APACHE.html.

10. See History of AOLServer at www.aolserver.com/docs/intro/history. html.

11. As stated by Michael Nelson in *The 2nd Workshop on the Open Archives Initiative (OAI): Gaining Independence with E-Prints Archives and OAI,* available at agenda.cern.ch/fullAgenda.php?ida=a02333.

12. Clifford Lynch, "Metadata Harvesting and the Open Archives Initiative," *ARL Bimonthly Report* 217 (August 2001). Available at www. arl.org/newsltr/217/mhp.html.

13. The suggestions come from one of the leading researchers in the digital libraries field, Dr. Edward Fox, at Virginia Tech. See the collection of papers at Digital Libraries in a Box—Annotated Bibliography at dlbox.nudl.org/pages/annotated_bibliography.html.

14. This initiative is described at UKOLN—Interoperability Focus—The Bath Profile at www.ukoln.ac.uk/interop-focus/bath/.

15. One of the many interesting aspects of this project is the combination of OAI and Z39.50 into one service. Described in Pete Cliff, "Building ResourceFinder," *Ariadne* 30 (December 2001). Available at www.ariadne.ac.uk/issue30/.

16. See the Library of Congress WWW/Z39.50 Gateway at www.loc. gov/z3950/gateway.html.

17. HubMed is an alternative, and highly regarded, interface for PubMed. For more information on it and its use of RSS, see www.pmbrowser. info/.

18. The project site for AmphetaDesk is at www.disobey.com/ amphetadesk/. It is a Perl-based application and uses a form of the Artistic License.

19. See, for example, the American Library Association page on the Patriot Act at www.ala.org/washoff/patriot.html.

Chapter 3

1. The main site for Adobe Photoshop is www.adobe.com/products/ photoshop/main.html.

2. See www.mostang.com/sane/.

3. A statement made about Pollo at pollo.sourceforge.net/. In fact, Pollo is an XML-tree editor, but a very good one, which is likely what inspired this claim.

4. Java might be second only to XML for sources. The official starting point is java.sun.com/. Java and XML are a good combination since they can be combined in so many different environments.

5. MathML is an XML-based standard for mathematical expressions. The MathML site is www.w3.org/Math/.

6. Found at www.openoffice.org/.

Chapter 4

1. The W3C site for XPath is at www.w3.org/TR/xpath.

2. See www.w3.org/TR/xptr.

3. The main AxKit site is at axkit.org/.

4. The best starting point for learning about mod_perl is "Welcome to the mod_perl World" at perl.apache.org/.

5. See the main Cocoon Web site at xml.apache.org/cocoon/.

6. The official site for SAX is www.saxproject.org/.

7. See "How to Publish XML Documents in HTML and PDF" at xml.apache.org/cocoon/howto/howto-html-pdf-publishing.html.

8. This is part of the Batik SVG Toolkit; see xml.apache.org/batik.

9. The W3C site for SVG is at www.w3.org/TR/SVG.

10. See the main site at digital.library.utoronto.ca/Tyrrell and technical details at digital.library.utoronto.ca/technical.html.

Chapter 5

1. A good starting point for learning more about Codd and the development of relational databases is at www.cciw.com/content/relationaldb.html.

2. Some vendors, such as Oracle, have special forms of BLOBs to handle text and other types of data.

3. The official MySQL site is at www.mysql.com.

4. See www.mysql.com.

Chapter 6

1. This is a distinction used by Ronald Bourret, a well-known XML database researcher, among others. A good starting point is "Defining XML Views over Relational Data" at www.rpbourret.com/xml/XMLViews.htm.

2. The official Zope site is at www.zope.org.

3. The ads can be distracting at ServerWatch, but "Application Servers" is a good example of the application class that this site excels at tracking the latest developments on. See www.serverwatch.com/stypes/.

4. PyXML is available from SourceForge at pyxml.sourceforge.net/.

5. The main 4Suite site is at 4suite.org.

6. Python is available at www.python.org.

7. ParsedXML is available in multiple versions, but the latest is at www.zope.org/Members/faassen/ParsedXML.

8. Available at www.zope.org/Members/arielpartners/XMLTransform/.

9. One of the consequences of the kind of free and collaborative environment found with OSS projects such as Zope is that several similar projects can go on simultaneously. XMLKit is described at www.zope.org/Members/haqa/XMLKit. Less ambitious than ParsedXML, XMLKit is much simpler to get running.

10. See the chapter entitled "Searching and Categorizing Content" at one of the versions of The Zope Book, which are maintained at www. zope.org/Documentation/Books/ZopeBook/.

11. This is currently taking shape on the Zope-xml list; see, for example, mail.zope.org/pipermail/zope-xml/2003-March/000328.html.

12. The official site for Xindice is xml.apache.org/xindice/.

13. Castor is an object/relational database mapping tool for XML. It is documented at castor.exolab.org. Note that Exolab no longer participates directly in its maintenance but continues to host the site and the mailing list.

14. Hibernate is available from SourceForge; see hibernate.sourceforge.net/. Not quite as mature as Castor, Hibernate is rapidly gaining ground as a similar mapping tool.

Chapter 7

1. OSS content management systems are numerous enough to have formed a nonprofit group to coordinate activities between projects called Open Source Content Management (OSCOM). See "OSCOM—Open Source Content Management" at www.oscom.org.

2. A good introduction to iVia can be found in Steve Mitchell, Margaret Mooney, Julie Mason, Gordon W. Paynter, Johannes Ruscheinski, Artur Kedzierski, and Keith Humphreys, "iVia Open Source Virtual Library System," D-Lib Magazine 9, no. 1 (January 2003). Available at www.dlib.org/dlib/january03/mitchell/01mitchell.html.

3. The starting point for dlbox is dlbox.nudl.org/pages/links.html.

4. See National Science Digital Library (NSDL) at nsdl.org.

5. See 5S Model/5S Language at www.dlib.vt.edu/projects/5S-Model.

6. MARIAN is not yet available, but has a Web site: www.dlib.vt.edu/products/marian.html.

7. A collection of readings on Fedora is available at www.iath.virginia.edu/sds/fedora.html.

8. Encoding systems such as ASCII assign numbers to characters. Prior to Unicode, no encoding system existed that could handle multiple languages, and there were sometimes conflicts between the number used for a character in one language and the same number used for a different character in another language. Unicode provides a unique

number for every character, regardless of the platform or language. The main Unicode Web site is www.unicode.org.

9. Found at www.nzdl.org.

10. Some demonstrations of Greenstone in action can be see at www. nzdl.org/cgi-bin/democols/library.

11. See Ian H. Witten, David Bainbridge, and Stefan J. Boddie, "Power to the People: End-User Building of Digital Library Collections," Proceedings of the First ACM/IEEE-CS Joint Conference on Digital Libraries, Roanoke, Va., January 2001, pp. 94–103.

12. SiteSearch can be found at www.sitesearch.oclc.org.

Chapter 8

1. There are, of course, many other alternatives to assembly language and C, such as PL/I and Fortran. Some might argue that C was a step back toward the hardware, but even the most readable of these alternatives comes up short against scripting languages.

2. One study involving 74 programmers at the University of Karlsruhe in Germany concluded that scripting takes about half the development effort when compared to Java, C, and C++. See John K. Ousterhout, "Scripting: Higher Level Programming for the 21st Century" at www.tcl. tk/doc/scripting.html.

3. TCL/TK can be utilized for many other functions as well; see www.tcl.tk. Note that Expect, the popular scripting environment for automating command-line functions is written in TCL. Expect can be found at expect.nist.gov.

4. JavaScript is not limited to browsers, though it is most commonly used there. Nombas and other companies sell environments for using JavaScript as a stand-alone application development system. See www.nombas.com.

5. Go to www.perl.com, the O'Reilly gathering point for all things related to Perl.

6. See www.cpan.org.

7. PHP is available at www.php.net.

8. Microsoft's ASP environment is mainly documented at the Microsoft Web site; see www.asp.net.

9. According to Netcraft's April 2002 survey, PHP is now the most deployed server-side scripting language, running on around 9 million of the 37 million sites in the survey. This is confirmed by PHP.net's own figures, which show PHP usage measured on a per-domain basis growing at approximately 5 percent per month. See www.netcraft.com/Survey/Reports/0204.

10. The official Python site is www.python.org.

11. See the brief history of regular expressions described at www.ercb.com/brief/brief.0041.html.

Chapter 9

1. See the Introduction in Daniel Greenstein and Suzanne E. Thorin, *The Digital Library: A Biography.* Available at www.clir.org/pubs/abstract/pub109abst.html.

2. The DLXS service is described at www.dlxs.org.

3. Stanford's digital library activities are described in Stanford Digital Library Technologies, available at www-diglib.stanford.edu/.

4. OCKHAM is an acronym for Open Component-based Knowledge Hypermedia Applications Management, and it has an official site hosted by Emory University; see ockham.library.emory.edu.

5. For information on CORBA, check the Object Management Group's official site, www.omg.org/.

6. The Enterprise JavaBeans specification is available at java.sun.com/products/ejb.

7. See the official NAICS site, www.census.gov/epcd/www/naics.html.

8. This is part of the mandate of the Web Services Description Working Group; see www.w3.org/2002/01/ws-desc-charter#mapping.

Chapter 10

1. The Perseus Digital Library can be found at www.perseus.tufts.edu.   The intent at one time was to make Perseus an open source distribution, but sites interested in the software should make queries through the site.

2. For VRML and other 3D technologies, go to the Web3D Consortium site www.web3d.org.

3. Starting at UNC, MyLibrary is now housed at Notre Dame; see dewey.library.nd.edu/mylibrary.

4. CMF stands for content management framework, and the main site for Zope's implementation is at the CMF Dogbowl; see cmf.zope.org/.

5. The main uPortal site is at freshmeat; see freshmeat.net/projects/uportal.

6. In the digital library world, this work is largely taking place at Virginia Tech; see the Open Digital Libraries site at oai.dlib.vt.edu/odl.

7. The Annozilla project site is annozilla.mozdev.org.

8. CYCLADES is documented at www.ercim.org/cyclades/.

9. See Jeff Rothenberg, *Avoiding Technological Quicksand: Finding a Viable Technical Foundation for Digital Preservation* (Council on Library and Information Resources, 1999).   Available at www.clir.org/pubs/reports/rothenberg/contents.html.

10. President's Information Technology Advisory Committee, *Digital Libraries: Universal Access to Human Knowledge* (2001). Available at www.ccic.gov/pubs/pitac/pitac-dl-9feb01.pdf.

11. The official LOCKSS site is lockss.stanford.edu.

12. DP9 can be found at arc.cs.odu.edu:8080/dp9/index.jsp.

13. See Internet Archive at www.archive.org.

14. The ISO site for OAIS is ssdoo.gsfc.nasa.gov/nost/isoas/ref_model.html.

15. The Cedars Project site is www.leeds.ac.uk/cedars/.

16. Institute of Museum and Library Services, *A Framework of Guidance for Building Good Digital Collections* (November 6, 2001).   Available at www.imls.gov/pubs/forumframework.htm.

17. Ibid.

Glossary

Adobe Illustrator (AI) A vector format for images created by Adobe and used by Photoshop and other Adobe applications.

AI. *See* Adobe Illustrator (AI)

AIFF. *See* Audio Interchange File Format (AIFF)

alphanumeric Usually refers to content created from a computer keyboard. In English, for example, content arising from the combined set of the 26 alphabetic characters, A to Z, the 10 Arabic numerals, 0 to 9, and other symbols available on a standard keyboard.

American Standard Code for Information Interchange (ASCII) A code for representing English characters as numbers, with each letter assigned a number from 0 to 127.

antialiasing Mostly applying to images, antialiasing involves adjusting pixel positions or intensities so that there is a more gradual transition between the color of a line and the background color. The term is also used with sound for a process of eliminating frequencies.

Apache Foundation A membership-based, not-for-profit corporation that seeks to ensure that Apache projects continue to exist beyond the participation of individual volunteers.

Applet A small, self-contained program that runs within a browser. Originally used only to designate applications that utilized a browser's Java Virtual Machine (therefore written in Java), *applet* is now sometimes used to generically identify any small program that runs inside another application.

Application A computer program or set of programs that carry out a defined set of functions.

archive Often used to describe a collection of the noncurrent records associated with an organization. This term is sometimes used to describe any collection of material, particularly digitized material, that is organized or brought together based on some criteria.

artifact A physical object made by human art and/or workmanship.

Artistic License One of the first OSS licenses and closely associated with Perl. The Artistic License allows for use in commercial applications.

ASCII. *See* American Standard Code for Information Interchange (ASCII)

Audio Interchange File Format (AIFF) Developed by Apple for storing high-quality sampled sound and musical instrument info. An extension, called AIFC or AIFF-C, supports compression.

authentication A process that ensures that an entity or object is what it claims to be.

authorization A process that assigns appropriate permission for carrying out activities such as accessing or modifying a resource.

bandwidth A measurement of how much data can be sent through a network at any one time.

Berkley System Distribution (BSD) license A license that formally recognizes that the copyright of the code belongs to the creators and will be promulgated to any derivative application.

binary A numbering scheme in which there are only two possible values for each digit: 0 and 1.

binary large object (BLOB) An object stored in a specific type of database field that goes beyond the capacity of other data types.

bitmap A map of "bits" that defines a display space and the color for each bit (usually referred to as a pixel).

BLOB. *See* binary large object (BLOB)

blog A short form of the term *weblog*. A blog is a journal or diary that is normally updated on a frequent basis and intended for general public consumption.

browser A client program to interact with the HTTP protocol.

BSD. *See* Berkley System Distribution (BSD) license

cache A temporary storage area that holds information that has already been accessed with the purpose of making that information faster to retrieve on subsequent requests. A cache is usually local or closer on a network to the user than the resources it holds in order to provide better response time.

cascading style sheets (CSS) A file or series of files for ornamenting HTML or XML-based content.

CGI. *See* Common Gateway Interface (CGI)

Common Gateway Interface (CGI) A specification for creating applications that supply dynamic content to Web browsers.

Common Object Request Broker Architecture (CORBA) An open network-based architecture and infrastructure that computer applications use to work together over networks.

compression A modified version of an object that is smaller because of a process or mechanism uses some method of removing information that can be recreated or approximated on request.

cookie Information from a Web site that the browser stores locally on a machine so that it can remember something about the user at a later time.

CORBA. *See* Common Object Request Broker Architecture (CORBA)

Creative Commons A form of licensing that generally is used for creative works, such as music.

crosswalk For metadata, a mapping between elements between two different schemes. For example, a crosswalk might specify that the author element of one scheme be considered the equivalent of the name element in another.

CSS. *See* cascading style sheets (CSS)

database A collection of data organized so that the contents can be accessed and managed easily.

digital library An organization or other formally structured entity that presides over digital collection(s).

Digital Library Federation (DLF) A federation comprising some of the largest research libraries and archives in the United States under the umbrella of the Council on Library and Information Resources (CLIR).

Digital Object Identifier (DOI) A unique and persistent alphanumeric ID for a resource.

digital signature A code used to ensure the integrity of a resource that relies on a special data element called a key, which normally can be supplied only by the owner of the signature.

DL. *See* digital library

DLF. *See* Digital Library Federation (DLF)

document type definition (DTD) A DTD states what elements are used to describe content in an SGML, XML, or HTML document. *See also* XML Schema

DOI. *See* Digital Object Identifier (DOI)

DTD. *See* document type definition (DTD)

Dublin Core A set of 15 metadata elements that are broad enough to be widely deployed.

EAD. *See* Encoded Archival Description (EAD)

EBCDIC. *See* Extended Binary-Coded Decimal Interchange Code

ECMAScript Derived from Netscape's JavaScript, the widely used scripting language support by Web browsers. ECMAScript was developed under the auspices of the European Computer Manufacturers Association (ECMA).

EJB. *See* Enterprise JavaBeans (EJB)

emulation A strategy for preservation in which a replica of the original computing environment is supplied to interact with a resource as intended by the creator(s) of the resource.

Encapsulated PostScript (EPS) An extension to PostScript language. EPS usually implies that the file contains a bit-mapped representation of the graphics for display purposes.

Encoded Archival Description (EAD) A standard for marking up the descriptive guides to archival holdings, often called Finding Aids. Originally defined as an SGML DTD, EAD is now available as an XML-DTD.

encryption A process of encoding information so that a special data element, called a key, is required to decode it.

Enterprise JavaBeans (EJB) An architecture from Sun Microsystems for using Java-based components.

EPS. *See* Encapsulated PostScript (EPS)

Extended Binary-Coded Decimal Interchange Code An IBM encoding scheme for Latin characters. This code has been supplanted largely by ASCII but is still found on mainframe computer systems.

Extensible Markup Language (XML) A subset of SGML, sharing with SGML the ability to create customized tags and enabling document validation.

Extensible Stylesheet Language (XSL) A powerful syntax for transforming XML content.

firewall A system that provides security for an organization by checking network traffic and denying access based on port numbers and other criteria.

fractal compression Works by identifying features in an image and modeling them as a series of repeating shapes and patterns. Fractals are a construct used to describe a structure that has many repeated forms. The math in fractal compression is complex enough to require a great amount of processing, but the benefits are up to 250:1 compression ratios.

freeware Software that is made freely available without a license and often without source code.

General Public License (GPL) A license that attempts to negate copyright so that a derivative work must continue to make the variations or additions in source code available.

GIF. *See* Graphics Interchange Format (GIF)

GNU A recursive acronym for GNU's not UNIX. The intent of the acronym was partially to distinguish between proprietary UNIX technologies and open source alternatives.

GNU Lesser General Public License. *See* Lesser General Public License (LGPL)

GPL. *See* General Public License (GPL)

Graphics Interchange Format (GIF) An image format that uses the LZW compression algorithm, owned by Unisys. To date, Unisys has not required users of GIF images to obtain a license, although its licensing statement indicates that it is a requirement. A patent-free alternative to GIF is PNG.

grid Utilizing the resources of many computers in a network for a single problem at the same time; using special software or arrangements that farm out pieces of a program to as many different machines as possible.

Handle A persistent identifier for a network resource.

HTML. *See* Hypertext Markup Language (HTML)

HTTP. *See* Hypertext Transfer Protocol (HTTP)

Hypertext Markup Language (HTML) An SGML-based markup language with a fixed set of tags.

Hypertext Transfer Protocol (HTTP) A stateless protocol that delivers content using MIME types.

IETF. *See* Internet Engineering Task Force (IETF)

IFF. *See* Audio Interchange File Format (AIFF)

interlaced Term commonly used with images. A process in which images "fade-in" in successive waves of lines until the entire image has completely arrived; this is a popular option for network-based display.

International Organisation for Standardization (ISO) A worldwide federation of national standards bodies from more than 140 countries. ISO's mission is to promote the development of standardization and related activities. The work of ISO results in international agreements that are published as International Standards.

Internet A global communications network consisting of thousands of interconnected networks.

Internet Engineering Task Force (IETF) An international community of network researchers that is open to any interested individual. It is the main standards organization for the Internet.

ISO. *See* International Organisation for Standardization (ISO)

Java A program environment from Sun Microsystems that provides a platform-independent basis for running applications.

Joint Photographic Experts Group (JPEG) An ISO/IEC group of experts that develops and maintains standards for a suite of compression algorithms for raster-based image files. Progressive JPEGs are interlaced images, and JPEG is a lossy format.

JPEG. *See* Joint Photographic Experts Group (JPEG)

Lempel-Ziv-Welch (LZW) compression A technique for compressing files that creates a list of bit patterns and substitutes a shorter code to save space.

Lesser General Public License (LGPL) A license that allows a charge to be levied when the source code is used in a commercial application. *See also* Artistic License

LGPL. *See* Lesser General Public License (LGPL)

Linux A complete, UNIX-like operating system that is the application most closely associated with the open source movement.

lossy Dropping some information from an image during compression. In many types of image compression, a small loss in quality is usually not noticeable, and dropping some information in the compression process can have a huge impact in the resulting file size.

LZW. *See* Lempel-Ziv-Welch (LZW) compression

metadata Popularly called "data about data." Metadata provides descriptive information about an object and/or its content.

migration A preservation strategy in which digital content is continually moved to new media in order to ensure it remains accessible.

MIME. *See* Multipurpose Internet Mail Extensions (MIME)

MIT License A BSD-style license that originates and covers many works at the Massachusetts Institute of Technology.

mono An open source implementation of Microsoft's .NET environment.

Moving Picture Experts Group (MPEG) An organization operating under ISO that defines formats for compressed audio and video files.

Mozilla Public License (MPL) A BSD-style license with special provision for reporting back changes/modifications to the source code to the license holders.

MPEG. *See* Moving Picture Experts Group (MPEG)

MPL. *See* Mozilla Public License (MPL)

MrSID A proprietary wavelet-based compression technology created by LizardTech (www.lizardtech.com/).

Multipurpose Internet Mail Extensions (MIME) An IETF specification for formatting non-ASCII messages so that they can be sent over the Internet.

namespace A URI that uniquely identifies a set of names so that there is no ambiguity when objects with different origins but the same names are mixed together. An XML namespace is usually a collection of element type and attribute names, though sometimes a namespace is a URI that doesn't point to a document and is used to delimit elements from others.

NCSA License From the University of Illinois/National Center for Supercomputing Application (NCSA). This license allows projects and applications originating with these organizations to utilize a BSD-style license.

.Net A Microsoft toolkit for Web services, integrated into most of its current application development tools.

Netscape Public License (NPL) A license that grants special rights to Netscape for server-side applications such that source code does not always have to be made available.

NPL. *See* Netscape Public License (NPL)

OAI. *See* Open Archives Initiative (OAI)

OCLC. *See* Online Computer Library Center (OCLC)

OCLC License A license that ensures modifications to source code are reported back to OCLC if the intent is to redistribute an application built with these modifications.

OCR. *See* optical character recognition (OCR)

Online Computer Library Center (OCLC) A nonprofit membership organization serving over 40,000 libraries in 86 countries and territories around the world.

ontology A controlled vocabulary for describing knowledge.

Open Archives Initiative (OAI) A project that develops and promotes interoperability standards for harvesting metadata from content repositories. OAI is also used to refer to the protocol used by the harvester called the Open Archives Initiative Protocol for Metadata Harvesting (OAI-PMH).

Open Source Initiative (OSI) A nonprofit corporation dedicated to managing and promoting the definition of *open source* for the public good.

open source license Allows software to be freely distributed with the source code, enabling the study, use, or modification of the software. OSI certifies OSS licenses deemed to be compatible with the goals of open source.

open source software (OSS) Generally used to designate software that includes the source code for the application and a license that governs its use.

OpenURL A URL that transports metadata or keys to access metadata for the object for which the OpenURL is provided.

optical character recognition (OCR) A process that converts scanned content to an ASCII or other character-orientated representation.

OSI. *See* Open Source Initiative (OSI)

OSS. *See* open source software (OSS)

PDF. *See* Portable Document Format (PDF)

Persistent Uniform Resource Locator (PURL) A URL that points to an intermediate resolution service, called a PURL server. This server redirects the user to the appropriate URL.

pixel Otherwise known as the "dot" in *dots per inch*. *Pixel* is a term that represents the "picture elements" that make up an image. The number of shades or colors a pixel can represent varies depending on the storage allocated for the image. The terms *ppi* and *pixels per inch* also refer to this storage capacity.

PNG. *See* Portable Graphics Format

Portable Document Format (PDF) A file format developed by Adobe Systems based on PostScript documents that allows them to appear on the recipient's monitor or printer as intended.

Portable Graphics Format A patent-free, compressed image format to replace GIF.

PostScript A language that treats the content of documents, including fonts, as collections of geometrical objects rather than bitmaps.

PURL. *See* Persistent Uniform Resource Locator (PURL)

QuickTime An audio/video format developed by Apple and recently licensed by MPEG.

Raster A grid of *x* and *y* coordinates on a display space, with a *z* coordinate for 3D images. A raster image file identifies which of these coordinates to illuminate in monochrome or color values.

RDBMS *See* relational database management system (RDBMS)

RDF. *See* Resource Description Framework (RDF)

relational database management system (RDBMS) A type of database that stores data in the form of related tables.

Resource Description Framework (RDF) A standard for processing metadata. RDF allows metadata to be used from several schemes together.

Semantic Web A broad description of a wide variety of technologies designed to add meaning to the Web.

SGML. *See* Standard Generalized Markup Language (SGML)

source code The programming statements that tell a computer or other automated system to perform functions in service of an application.

SQL. *See* Standard Query Language (SQL)

Standard Generalized Markup Language (SGML) A system that allows elements of a document to be organized and tagged.

Standard Query Language (SQL) A query language for requesting information from a database.

streaming The process of downloading enough of a file so that a viewer or "player" can stay just ahead of the download with no interruption in viewing or hearing.

Tagged Image Format (TIFF) An open, raster-based file format originally developed by Aldus and Microsoft.

TEI. *See* Text Encoding Initiative (TEI)

Text Encoding Initiative (TEI) A widely supported standard for encoding machine-readable texts of interest in the humanities and social sciences. Originally defined in SGML, TEI has made the transition to XML and is considered the de facto standard for encoding literary and linguistics texts, corpora, and the like.

TIFF. *See* Tagged Image File Format (TIFF)

Unicode An encoding scheme that seeks to assign a single number for all characters in all the written languages of the world. Unicode currently employs a scheme that can handle over a million characters.

vector image file Graphics that use commands or mathematical statements to place lines and shapes in a given two-dimensional or three-dimensional space. This has great advantages for file storage. Instead of containing a bit in the file for each bit of a line drawing, a vector graphic file describes a series of points to be connected. Vector images are usually converted into raster graphics images for display.

W3C. *See* World Wide Web Consortium (W3C)

watermark Embedded copyright information within an object, usually through a symbol or other visual symbol.

wavelet A mathematical modeling method that breaks an image down by identifying shapes and patterns. Using complex math, wavelet-based techniques can achieve up to 150:1 compression ratios.

Windows operating systems Software originally released in 1985 to act as an interface to MS-DOS. Now it refers to a series of operating systems from Microsoft. The term *windows* is sometimes used to refer to any graphical interface used for a computer application.

World Wide Web (WWW) The collection of resources available on the Internet that are accessible using HTTP.

World Wide Web Consortium (W3C) Created in October 1994. The W3C develops interoperable technologies for use on the Web and oversees a volunteer standards process. W3C has approximately 450 member organizations from all over the world, including the Library of Congress and OCLC.

WWW. *See* World Wide Web (WWW)

X Bitmap Format (XBM) A native file format of the X Window.

XBM. *See* X Bitmap Format (XBM)

XHTML The XML specification for HTML tags. It is generally used as a way to take advantage of the many XML toolkits now available and also to act as a bridge for legacy documents currently marked up in HTML.

XML. *See* Extensible Markup Language (XML)

XML Schema The successor to DTDs. XML Schema uses XML instead of the more cryptic syntax of DTDs to specify which elements are allowed in a document.

XPath A standard that describes a way to locate items in an XML document based on the document's logical structure.

XPointer A language for locating data within an XML document.

XSL. *See* Extensible Stylesheet Language (XSL)

Z39.50 A widely supported ANSI/NISO standard for searching and information retrieval.

Further Resources:
Digital Library and Open
Source Resources on the Web

Starting Points: Digital Libraries

A Framework of Guidance for Building Good Digital Collections at www.imls.
gov/pubs/forumframework.htm
> From the Institute of Museum and Library Services, this is an invaluable resource for building digital collections.

Ariadne at www.ariadne.ac.uk/
> Ariadne is published every three months by the United Kingdom Office of Library Networking (UKOLN). In addition to news and commentary on digital library initiatives and technologies, Ariadne includes content on general library and information technology developments, all with a very practical perspective.

BUBL LINK 025.0 Digital Libraries and Online Services at link.bubl.ac.uk/
digitallibraries/
> BUBL LINK is a catalogue of selected Internet resources covering all academic subject areas organized around Dewey decimal classification (DDC). Links are checked and fixed on a monthly basis, no small feat considered the size of this site.

Berkeley Digital Library SunSITE at sunsite.berkeley.edu/
> A great collection of tools and collections for digital library projects and home to the archives of the Web4Lib and XML4Lib listservs, two active and very useful mailing lists for digital library managers.

CLIR Issues at www.clir.org/pubs/issues/issues.html
> CLIR is an independent, nonprofit organization that serves as the administrative home to the Digital Library Federation. CLIR seeks to ensure that information resources needed by scholars, students, and the general public are available for future generations, and this bimonthly publication never fails to deliver provoking commentary and information on digital library projects.

D-Lib Magazine at www.dlib.org/
    Sponsored by the Defense Advanced Research Project Agency (DARPA) with funding by the National Science Foundation (NSF), *D-Lib Magazine* is published 11 times a year by the Corporation for National Research Initiatives (CNRI) and features leading-edge articles and briefs on digital library research and development.

Digital Libraries at www.cs.cornell.edu/wya/DigLib/
    The online version of William Y. Arms's quintessential work on digital libraries.

Digital Libraries Initiative Phase Two at www.dli2.nsf.gov/
    The Digital Libraries Initiative Phase Two is a project funded by the National Science Foundation and other high-profile organizations to provide leadership in research fundamental to the continued development of digital libraries. The reports from the various working committees associated with this initiative alone make this resource worth visiting, but it is also a tool for tracking the impressive range of DLI workshops.

Digital Library Federation Home Page at www.diglib.org/dlfhomepage.htm
    In particular, see the Publications section. The DLF represents the leading institutions working in digital libraries in the United States and is a focal point for DL research.

Digital Library Information and Resources at bengross.com/dl/
    A regularly updated list of annotated resources maintained by Ben Gross, a researcher and scholar who coordinates the Digital Libraries Initiative Phase Two for the National Science Foundation.

eCulture at www.cordis.lu/ist/ka3/digicult/newsletter.htm
    Originating with the European Commission's Information Society Technologies program, this bimonthly publication is useful for staying up-to-date on European activity on digital libraries, particularly in terms of upcoming conferences.

Interactive Digital Library Resource System (i-DLR) at tiger.coe.missouri.edu/ ~rafee/iDLR/index.php
    i-DLR was initiated by a group of graduate students in the School of Information Science and Learning Technologies (SISLT), University of Missouri-Columbia in 2000 and has been kept up-to-date by several groups and students since that time. A comprehensive digital library in its own right, i-DLR is an excellent entry point to a rapidly growing field.

Journal of Digital Information at jodi.ecs.soton.ac.uk/
    A peer-reviewed Web journal supported by the British Computer Society and Oxford University Press that is currently free to access. Digital libraries

and other topics on the management, presentation, and uses of information in digital environments are addressed.

RLG DigiNews at www.rlg.org/preserv/diginews/
Produced for the Research Libraries Group by Cornell University Libraries Department of Preservation and Conservation, *RLG DigiNews* is a bimonthly newsletter focusing on issues of interest for digital library initiatives.

Scholarly Electronic Publishing Bibliography/6.2 Library Issues: Digital Libraries at info.lib.uh.edu/sepb/lbdiglib.htm
The Digital Libraries section of Charles W. Bailey, Jr.'s well-known and highly regarded bibliography.

Standards for Digital Information Interchange. A Resources Page at ahds.ac.uk/interchange.htm
The Arts and Humanities Data Service (AHDS) is a U.K. national service to collect, preserve, and promote reuse of the digital content that results from research in the arts and humanities. The site includes information on AHDS and other workshops.

Unicode at www.unicode.org
The main starting point to learn about Unicode, this site includes good introductory materials.

Starting Points: Open Source Software

Apache at www.apache.org
The home page of the Apache Foundation and the central point for its many OSS projects, including the Web server application that gives most of the Web its foundation for existence.

freshmeat at freshmeat.net
freshmeat is possibly the Web's largest index of open source software, though it does include some commercial packages. If you want to find an OSS option for any conceivable computer application, freshmeat is a good starting point.

oss4lib at oss4lib.org
The main OSS site for the library community, maintained by Dan Chudnov at Yale University, the leading spokesperson for the use of open source software by and for libraries.

Slashdot at slashdot.org/
A gathering point for OSS advocates, dissenters, and almost every other conceivable segment of the computing population, slashdot is a fascinating glimpse of programmers and application users in dialogue on topics that vary from code quality to moral issues.

sourceforge at sourceforge.net
> sourceforge offers a suite of services for OSS projects and developers, including disk space, provision for downloading from mirror sites all over the world, and mailing list support. It is the preferred site for making an OSS application available.

Selected Collections and Projects

Alexandria Digital Library Project at alexandria.ucsb.edu/
> A distributed digital library for geographically referenced information, this project offers unique interfaces for geospatial data.

American Memory Project at memory.loc.gov
> The biggest and most comprehensive digital library project in active operation, containing more than 7 million digital items from more than 100 historical collections at the time of this writing.

ARL Digital Initiatives Database at www.arl.org/did/
> The ARL Digital Initiatives Database is a collaboration between the University of Illinois at Chicago and the American Research Libraries group to maintain a registry for descriptions of digital initiatives in or involving libraries. At the time of this writing, the registry contained close to 450 entries.

arXiv.org e-Print archive at arxiv.org/
> An e-print service that dates back to 1991, arXiv.org contains research papers in the fields of physics, mathematics, nonlinear science, and computer science.

Canada's Digital Collections at collections.ic.gc.ca/
> This site contains a collection of projects from Canada, from the very small to the very large.

Canadian Initiative on Digital Libraries (CIDL) at www.nlc-bnc.ca/cidl/
> An alliance of Canadian libraries that seeks collaboration on the use of digital information and related services. Links to best practices in creating and presenting digital content in Canada and elsewhere are available on this Web site.

Corpus of Electronic Texts (CELT) at www.ucc.ie/celt/
> Focusing on Irish literary and historical culture (in Irish, Latin, Anglo-Norman French, and English), CELT grew out of a project of the Department of History and the Computer Centre at University College Cork in Cork, Ireland. English translations are provided as available for the many historical materials at this site.

Gallica at gallica.bnf.fr/
> The Bibliothèque Nationale de France's Gallica Web site offers unique resources from its own collection.

HALINET at www.halinet.on.ca/
> A partnership of several Ontario educational institutions, HALINET is a unique intersection of current and historical materials, many of which have been digitized on a volunteer basis.

National Library of Australia (NLA) Pictures Catalogue at www.nla.gov.au/ catalogue/pictures/
> The successor to NLA's highly regarded Images1 collection, this site contains stunning pictures from a stunning landscape.

NCSA Astronomy Digital Image Library (ADIL) at imagelib.ncsa.uiuc.edu/ imagelib.html
> A fascinating and interactive site, ADIL makes good use of VRML and 3D for astronomical, research-quality images.

Networked Computer Science Technical Reference Library (NCSTRL) at www. ncstrl.org/
> NCSTRL is an international collection of computer science technical reports from computer science departments and public/private-sector research laboratories, made available for noncommercial and educational use. Powered by Arc (see OAI Systems).

Networked Digital Library of Theses and Dissertations (NDLTD) at www. ndltd.org
> In 1996, Virginia Tech developed tools for students to submit theses and dissertations as both SGML and PDF documents. In 1998, the University of West Virginia used these tools to implement the requirement that all theses and dissertations be submitted online in Electronic Thesis and Dissertation (ETD) format. NDLTD now represents over 100 member institutions.

New Zealand Digital Library at www.nzdl.org/cgi-bin/library
> A broad range of collections on largely global topics. This site is a showcase site for Greenstone in action.

Perseus Project at www.perseus.tufts.edu/
> One of the most fascinating and unique digital library systems available, the focus of Perseus is on the ancient Greek and Roman world, though the project's underlying tools have been used for other collections that are linked to the site. Unfortunately, the tools used for Perseus are not yet open source, though Tufts University, which manages the site, seems very amenable to working with other institutions on digital collections.

Research in Virtual Reality Digital Libraries at www.dlib.vt.edu/products/
VRDL.html
> From the Digital Library Research Laboratory at Virginia Tech, a col-
lection of projects that give a glimpse of the next generation of digital library development.

University of Michigan Digital Library Project at www.si.umich.edu/UMDL/
> This is an always-interesting collection of updates and demonstration
technologies from one of the first large digital library projects.

University of New Brunswick Electronic Text Centre at www.lib.unb.ca/Texts/
> In addition to historical collections, this Text Centre also publishes
several current scholarly journals.

University of Virginia Electronic Text Center at etext.lib.virginia.edu
> This is an amazing set of collections and images from around the
world, but with special emphasis on the American South.

Vatican Library at bav.vatican.va/en/
> Anyone around computers during the early days of the Web will re-
member the Vatican Library being a groundbreaking digital collection for
the Web.

Measuring Use

D-Lib Working Group on Digital Library Metrics at www.dlib.org/metrics/public/
> The documents and position papers assembled at this site bring to-
gether some of the leading thinkers on digital libraries.

E-Metrics: Measures for Electronic Resources at www.arl.org/stats/newmeas/
emetrics/
> This is the Association of Research Libraries page on measuring the
use and value of electronic resources.

Metadata

Dublin Core Metadata Initiative at dublincore.org/
> This is the official site for Dublin Core activities and a great starting
point.

Encoded Archival Description (EAD) at www.loc.gov/ead/
> Another standard maintained by the Network Development and
MARC Standards Office of the Library of Congress, this time in partnership with the Society of American Archivists. EAD is the most widely deployed standard to consult for finding aids and archival collections.

Federal Geographic Data Committee (FGDC) at www.fdgc.gov
    This is the place to go if you are working with cartographic objects such as maps for your collection.

IFLANET Metadata Resources at www.ifla.org/II/metadata.htm
    From the International Federation of Library Associations and Institutions (IFLA), this site contains numerous resources on many metadata initiatives, particularly Dublin Core and MARC.

Introduction to Metadata at www.getty.edu/research/institute/standards/intrometadata
    A project funded by the J. Paul Getty Trust, this online publication is an excellent starting point for metadata newbies.

MARC Standards at www.loc.gov/marc/
    From the Network Development and MARC Standards Office of the Library of Congress, this is the official starting point for all things related to MARC. It includes some great introductory material along with the latest developments, including the Library of Congress projects to bring together MARC and XML.

MetaMap at www.mapageweb.umontreal.ca/turner/meta/english/
    Using SVG to construct a subway map. MetaMap shows the relationship between metadata standards. A must-see for those interested in metadata or SVG.

Resource Description Framework (RDF) at www.w3.org/RDF/
    This is the official page for RDF and the starting point to many related standards.

TAP at tap.stanford.edu/
    This is an intriguing standard and application from some very big players in the digital library world.

Text Encoding Initiative (TEI) at www.tei-c.org/
    This is the starting point for TEI, an essential standard for any digital collections dealing with text.

TopicMaps.org at www.topicmaps.org/xtm/
    TopicMaps.org is an independent organization and maintains the XML family of specifications for topic maps. The main XML topic maps standard is a model for how to write a readable standard.

UKOLN Metadata at www.ukoln.ac.uk/metadata/
    The UKOLN participates in or tracks many metadata projects, and this list reflects an active engagement in metadata issues.

W3C Semantic Web Activity at www.w3.org/2001/sw/
> Despite the *2001* in the URL, this is a very active site and an area of focus for the W3C. Links to many Semantic Web–related standards and publications.

XOBIS at xobis.stanford.edu
> Probably the most ambitious MARC/XML integration project in existence, XOBIS comes out of the Lane Medical Library at Stanford University and attempts to forge new frontiers for MARC by rethinking how it is used.

MySQL

Database Journal's MySQL Articles at www.databasejournal.com/features/mysql/
> This site offers in-depth articles on both basic and advanced topics for using MySQL.

MySQL Related Sites at www.mysql.com/portal/sites/index.html
> From the MySQL site, this page provides categorized listings of MySQL resources.

SQLCourse at sqlcourse.com/
> This is an interactive tutorial that is not specific to MySQL but that offers a good entry point for learning SQL before diving into the system.

OAI

Open Archives Initiative at www.openarchives.org/
> This is the main starting point for OAI, including links to the OAI systems covered in Chapter 2, as well as information on related conferences and the most current version of the OAI protocol standard.

Budapest Open Access Initiative at www.soros.org/openaccess/
> Arising from a meeting convened in Budapest by the Open Society Institute (OSI) in December 2001, this initiative seeks to accelerate progress in the international effort to make research articles in all academic fields freely available on the internet. The initiative has been signed by the Budapest participants and a growing number of individuals and organizations representing every segment of the public and scholarly community.

DSpace at www.dspace.org
>A joint project of MIT Libraries and the Hewlett-Packard Company, DSpace is a scalable repository system suitable for midsized to large collections and organizations.

EPrints at www.eprints.org/
>More Perl-centric compared to DSpace's Java focus, EPrints was one of the first large-scale projects to be used to house the research output of an organization.

Preservation

CAMiLEON at www.si.umich.edu/CAMILEON/
>Creative Archiving at Michigan and Leeds: Emulating the Old on the New (CAMiLEON) is a joint project between the Universities of Michigan (U.S.) and Leeds (U.K.) to investigate the use of emulation as a digital preservation strategy.

CEDARS at www.leeds.ac.uk/cedars/
>The CURL Exemplars in Digital Archives project investigates strategies that will ensure that digital information resources be preserved over the longer term. Managed by the Consortium of University Research Libraries (CURL), the CEDARS project has created some very valuable project reports, particularly in terms of scoping out OAIS for preservation metadata.

OCLC/RLG Preservation Metadata Working Group at www.oclc.org/research/pmwg/
>This group has published two comprehensive reports that reflect the impressive roster of members. The working group, in fact, is now made up of two groups, one charged with examining preservation metadata, and the other with implementation strategies.

Preserving Access to Digital Information (PADI) at www.nla.gov.au/padi/
>The National Library of Australia has been a leader in digital preservation and maintains an extensive site on preservation topics.

Scripting

cgi-bin.com at www.cgi-bin.com/
>This site is ad-heavy, but contains a huge collection of example scripts for PHP and Perl.

DevShed: The Open Source Web Development Site at www.devshed.com/
An excellent source of tutorials and real-life examples for open source applications. Perl, PHP, Python, MySQL, and Zope are all given sections on this site, and it has many introductory articles.

WebMonkey at hotwired.lycos.com/webmonkey/index.html
If you can see past the outrageous color schemes, there is a lot of good information on this site for building Web sites and services with scripts.

Web Services

Simple Object Access Protocol (SOAP) at www.soapware.org/
There are many Web resources for SOAP, but this is a very well-maintained and comprehensive directory for SOAP specifications and implementations.

Uniform Description, Discovery, and Integration (UDDI) at www.uddi.org
UDDI seems to be the hardest sell for Web services, which has been overwhelmed by hype in almost every other aspect. The concept of distributed registries of services is an important one for digital libraries, UDDI may provide some useful plumbing for building services for digital collections even if it doesn't become widely accepted within the software industry.

Web Service Definition Language (WSDL) at www.w3.org/TR/wsdl
A submission to the W3C, WSDL is not a W3C-endorsed standard (note the *TR* in the URL, which refers to technical documents held by the W3C). This document is a good overview of how WSDL works.

XML

Cover Pages: Core Standards at xml.coverpages.org/coreStandards.html
This is a clearinghouse for XML standards and projects from OASIS.

XML.com at xml.com
This is a comprehensive XML site actively maintained by O'Reilly & Associates.

XML for Libraries at escholarship.cdlib.org/rtennant/presentations/2002cil
This is a presentation on XML from one of the library community's leading practitioners.

Z39.50

Z39.50 Maintenance Agency Page at www.loc.gov/z3950/agency/
> The main site for Z39.50 at the Library of Congress. The best starting point for viewing the protocol, though the software list is not complete.

Cheshire II at cheshire.lib.berkeley.edu/

Isite at www.cnidr.org/isite.html

JAFER at www.lib.ox.ac.uk/jafer/

Zebra at www.indexdata.dk/zebra/

Zope

Build a Searchable Job Board at www.zope.org/Members/mukhsein/job_board_howto
> This site provides a good example of how a complete application can be built in Zope using its object database and an excellent starting point for appreciating the power of Zope.

The Zope Book at www.zope.org/Documentation/Books/ZopeBook/current/
> The most up-to-date version of this comprehensive reference on Zope can be found here.

Index

157